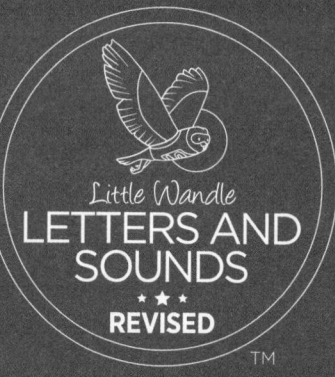

Teacher's Guide
SEND Programme:
Graduated Approach

William Collins' dream of knowledge for all began with the publication of his first book in 1819.
A self-educated mill worker, he not only enriched millions of lives, but also founded a flourishing publishing house. Today, staying true to this spirit, Collins books are packed with inspiration, innovation and practical expertise.
They place you at the centre of a world of possibility and give you exactly what you need to explore it.

Collins. Freedom to teach.

Published by Collins

An imprint of HarperCollins*Publishers*
The News Building, 1 London Bridge Street, London, SE1 9GF, UK

HarperCollins*Publishers*
1st Floor, Watermarque Building, Ringsend Road, Dublin 4, Ireland

Browse the complete Collins catalogue at
collins.co.uk

© Wandle Learning Trust 2022
www.littlewandlelettersandsounds.org.uk

10 9 8 7 6 5 4 3 2 1

ISBN 978-0-00-858260-9

British Library Cataloguing-in-Publication Data
A catalogue record for this publication is available from the British Library.

Authors: Charlotte Raby and Catherine Baker
Publisher: Lizzie Catford
Copyeditor: Tracy Kewley
Proofreader: Jennie Clifford
Cover designer: Steve Evans
Internal designer and typesetter: Pascal Don
Illustrator: Noah Warnes
Production controller: Katharine Willard
Printed and Bound in the UK using 100% Renewable Electricity at Martins the Printers Ltd.

Thank you to Christine Perkins, Beatrice Durston and all the special schools that were part of the Little Wandle SEND forum for their help with the development of the Little Wandle SEND programme.

Extracts from the *SEND code of practice: 0 to 25 years* (DfE 2014), *The engagement model* (STA 2020), *The reading framework* (DfE 2022) and the *Education inspection framework* (Ofsted 2019) are reproduced under the terms of the Open Government Licence (OGL) v3.0. www.nationalarchives.gov.uk/doc/open-government-licence/version/3.

This book is produced from independently certified FSC™ paper to ensure responsible forest management.

For more information visit:
www.harpercollins.co.uk/green

Wandle Learning Trust and Little Sutton Primary School have partnered with HarperCollins*Publishers* to provide teachers with a full systematic synthetic phonics programme, *Little Wandle Letters and Sounds Revised*, and accompanying Collins Big Cat readers. Full details of the programme, including CPD training, can be found at www.littlewandlelettersandsounds.org.uk.

Contents

A downloadable version of this guide is available at collins.co.uk/SENDProgrammeTeacherGuide/download

Introducing the Little Wandle SEND programme

We want to teach every child to read!

Learning to read matters for every child or young person, regardless of their starting points or learning needs. This is why *Little Wandle Letters and Sounds Revised* offers a number of pathways, enabling schools to create a suitable route to reading for every child.

Little Wandle SEND (special educational needs and disabilities) is a complete programme that mirrors the main *Little Wandle Letters and Sounds Revised* phonics programme but with adaptations and support in place that make it possible for schools, special schools and providers to meet the needs of all their learners.

It has been created to help children learn to read using the right level of challenge for each child and using the graduated approach if needed. This quote from the Reading framework makes it clear why this is so important:

'Children (with SEND) have to navigate the same written language, unlock the same alphabetic code, learn the same skills, and learn and remember the same body of knowledge as their peers. It is a critical skill in helping them prepare for adulthood.' (*The reading framework: Teaching the foundations of literacy*, DfE 2021)

In addition to this Teacher's guide, the Little Wandle SEND programme includes:

Printed resources from Collins – created specifically for the SEND programme:
- Word cards and tricky word cards for all phases
- Grapheme cards with images for Phase 5
- Large sensory grapheme cards for Phases 2, 3 and 5
- Large desktop Grapheme mat for Phases 2, 3 and 5.

Decodable books from Collins:
- 204 fully decodable books
- 50 new 7+ decodable books, including 10 blending practice books for Phases 2 and 3.

In the SEND area of the Little Wandle website at www.littlewandlelettersandsounds.org.uk:
- Assessment tools
- Weekly grids
- 'How to' videos
- A range of other teaching resources including image banks for Phases 2 to 5
- Training and continuing professional development (CPD): In order to deliver Little Wandle SEND, teachers must be fully trained in both the initial Little Wandle training and the specific SEND training. All the training is available to members in the CPD area of the website.

Little Wandle SEND has been trialled in special schools with children who have a wide range of learning and physical disabilities, so that we can be sure that it provides the support needed to develop children's language as well as teaching them how to read words.

Choosing the correct programme for children below age-related expectations in reading

There will be children in your school or setting who have not yet learned to read or are taking longer than their peers. All children who are reading at below the expected level for their age should be assessed immediately to identify what support and teaching they need to become fluent, accurate readers. For each child, you need to consider carefully which Little Wandle teaching programme they need: SEND, Keep-up or Rapid catch-up.

SEND

You should teach and support any child that has a SEND that requires adaptations and slower pace, due to cognitive function or other disabilities, through the Little Wandle SEND programme. If they do not have a specific SEND that requires adjustments or adaptations, then the main programme Keep-up or Rapid catch-up are most likely to meet their needs.

Some children with SEND will require very few or very small adaptations to the main Little Wandle programme (to meet their sensory needs, for example). Other children will need fundamental changes to the pace and progression of the programme to meet their more complex needs. The information on pages 14 to 17 will support you in identifying the correct pathway for individuals with SEND.

Keep-up

The Little Wandle Keep-up programme is designed to help children in Reception and Year 1 who at are at risk of falling behind their peers to keep up. Children following *Little Wandle Letters and Sounds Revised* who do not have a SEND should be given support in the form of one-to-one or group keep-up sessions. (See the Keep-up area of the Little Wandle website for further information.)

Some elements of the Keep-up programme will also be useful for children with SEND who are able to access the main Little Wandle programme with few or small adaptations – see Pathway 1 on page 15.

Rapid catch-up

The Little Wandle Rapid catch-up programme is for children in Year 2 and above who are not meeting age-related expectations in reading. It is designed to help children catch up rapidly and covers the Little Wandle progression at a faster pace. Children in Year 2 who need support with reading but do not have a SEND may benefit from the Rapid catch-up programme. See the Rapid catch-up area of the Little Wandle website for further information, and use the Rapid catch-up assessment materials to check whether this programme would be appropriate for an individual child.

Foundations for phonics

The Little Wandle SEND programme is designed for children in Reception and above who are ready to learn phonics. Support for Early Years children with SEND – 'Foundations for phonics: Tuning into sounds' – can be found in the SEND area of the Little Wandle website.

Guidance for special schools, bases and specialist providers

Little Wandle and the SEND Code of Practice

The SEND Code of Practice (2014) is a statutory framework and therefore it is a legal requirement for all special schools and specialist providers. It supports the use of reasonable adjustments and aids to ensure children with disabilities get all the support they need to access education. This gives special schools the mandate to make adjustments to materials needed for teaching in order to meet the needs of their pupils.

For special schools following *Little Wandle Letters and Sounds Revised*, making adjustments might mean using adapted resources, cued articulation, British Sign Language (BSL), Makaton, eye gazes, Picture Exchange Communication System (PECS) or other adjustments that enable children to learn to read using the Little Wandle programme.

Children who are blind or partially sighted can access free adapted versions of the Little Wandle resources and books from the RNIB. Go to www.rnibbookshare.org and search for 'Little Wandle'.

Making adjustments might also involve adaptations to the pace and progression of the Little Wandle programme. Some children will not need the progression or teaching of the programme adapted except in very small ways (to meet their sensory needs, for example). Other children will need fundamental changes to the pace and progression of the programme to meet their more complex needs. (See page 14 for advice on determining the correct pathway for each child.)

All children with SEND can be supported using the graduated approach, as described by the Code of Practice (2014), through small-step teaching to the point of challenge. See 'Using the graduated approach with Little Wandle' on page 30. The SEND assessment shows progress for children in smaller steps, and you can record your planning for small-step teaching on the 'Individual progress' document, available in the SEND area of the Little Wandle website.

The importance of reasonable adjustments

The SEND Code of Practice (2014), the Equality Act (2010) and Section 21 of the Children and Families Act (2014) all ensure that children's individual needs are planned for. Teaching children with complex needs does mean that, for many, theirs will be a specific and personalised curriculum to match their cognitive requirements. This could mean more repetition, shorter lessons, more sensory input etc.

There is no expectation for pupils to be taught as a whole class (as in the main Little Wandle programme). Rather, individual paths of progress need to be created that follow the Little Wandle progression and a direct-instruction approach, modified to create challenge and ensure progress for each child.

Parental involvement is key and should be part of the provision – this is especially important for children learning to read.

Extracts from the SEND Code of Practice

The following extracts from the SEND Code of Practice (2014) will be useful for teachers planning phonics provision for individuals with SEND.

'They [schools and providers] must make reasonable adjustments, including the provision of auxiliary aids and services, to ensure that disabled children and young people are not at a substantial disadvantage compared with their peers. This duty is anticipatory – it requires thought to be given in advance to what disabled children and young people might require and what adjustments might need to be made to prevent that disadvantage.'

'The principles [underpinning the Code of Practice] are designed to support:
- high quality provision to meet the needs of children and young people with SEN
- a focus on inclusive practice and removing barriers to learning
- successful preparation for adulthood, including independent living and employment.'

'High quality teaching that is differentiated and personalised will meet the individual needs of the majority of children and young people. Some children and young people need educational provision that is additional to or different from this. This is special educational provision under Section 21 of the Children and Families Act 2014. Schools and colleges must use their best endeavours to ensure that such provision is made for those who need it. Special educational provision is underpinned by high quality teaching and is compromised by anything less.

Early Years providers, schools and colleges should know precisely where children and young people with SEN are in their learning and development. They should:
- ensure decisions are informed by the insights of parents and those of children and young people themselves
- have high ambitions and set stretching targets for them
- track their progress towards these goals
- keep under review the additional or different provision that is made for them
- promote positive outcomes in the wider areas of personal and social development, and
- ensure that the approaches used are based on the best possible evidence and are having the required impact on progress.'

From the section 'High quality provision to meet the needs of children and young people with SEN'

'Where a setting identifies a child as having SEN, they must work in partnership with parents to establish the support the child needs.'

'All settings should adopt a graduated approach with four stages of action: assess, plan, do and review.'

'These areas [communication and interaction, cognition and learning, social, emotional and mental health, sensory and/or physical needs] give an overview of the range of needs that providers should plan for. However, individual children often have needs that cut across all these areas and their needs may change over time. For instance, speech, language and communication needs can also be a feature of a number of other areas of SEN, and children with an Autism Spectrum Condition may have needs across all areas. The special educational provision made for a child should always be based on an understanding of their particular strengths and needs and should seek to address them all, using well-evidenced interventions targeted at areas of difficulty and, where necessary, specialist equipment or software. This will help to overcome barriers to learning and participation. Support should be family centred and should consider the individual family's needs and the best ways to support them.'

From the section 'Improving outcomes: high aspirations and expectations for children with SEN'

Little Wandle for pupils at pre-Key Stage 1 levels

Schools with children who are working below the Key Stage 1 levels (or pre-levels) should be following the engagement model as set out by the DfE in *The engagement model: Guidance for maintained schools, academies (including free schools) and local authorities* (DfE 2020).

You should also refer to the teacher assessment framework for pre-Key Stage 1 – provided for the statutory assessment of pupils engaged in subject-specific study who are working below the overall standard of the National Curriculum tests and teacher assessment frameworks. See *Pre-key stage 1: pupils working below the national curriculum assessment standard: Teacher assessment framework* (DfE 2020).

The framework guidance for teachers states:

'These standards are not a formative assessment tool: they should not be used to track progress throughout the key stage or to guide individual programmes of study, classroom practice or methodology. Teachers should assess individual pieces of pupils' work in line with their school's own, more detailed, assessment policy and not against these standards. Those reviewing school performance, including Ofsted inspectors, would not expect them to be used for anything other than summative assessment at the end of the key stage.

The pre-key stage standards may also be useful for teachers to refer to for pupils of all ages, including those attending secondary school, but there is no statutory requirement to do so.'

The pre-key stage standards focus clearly on specific aspects of the English reading curriculum, which is useful to consider when thinking about whether a child is ready to engage with and benefit from phonics teaching, as well as how children who make slower progress can be assessed in a more summative way.

Pre-key stage standards for English language comprehension and reading

Standard 1
Language comprehension In a familiar story/rhyme, the pupil can, when being read to by an adult (one-to-one or in a small group): • indicate correctly pictures of the characters and objects in response to questions such as 'Where is (the)…?' • show anticipation about what is going to happen (e.g. by turning the page) • join in with some actions or repeat some words, rhymes or phrases when prompted.

Children who are at Standard 1 do not need phonics instruction. Use the Foundations for phonics activities (on the Little Wandle website) to grow phonemic awareness and develop listening skills. Standard 2 relates to any Phase 2 GPC that the child has secured.

Standard 2

Word reading[1]

The pupil can:
- say a single sound for 10+ graphemes
- read words by blending sounds with known graphemes, with help from their teacher.

Language comprehension

In a familiar story/rhyme, the pupil can, when being read to by an adult (one-to-one or in a small group):
- demonstrate understanding, e.g. by answering questions, such as 'Where is he/she/it?', 'What time is this?', 'Who is this?', 'What is he/she doing?'
- join in with predictable phrases or refrains.

[1]At Standard 2 only, teachers can consider the small number of pupils who can read words as 'sight words' to have met the word reading statements.

Standard 3

Word reading

The pupil can:
- say a single sound for 20+ graphemes
- read accurately by blending sounds with two and three known graphemes.

Language comprehension

In a familiar story/rhyme, the pupil can, when being read to by an adult (one-to-one or in a small group):
- respond to questions that require simple recall
- recount a short sequence of events (e.g. by sequencing images or manipulating objects).

Standard 4

Word reading

The pupil can:
- say a single sound for 40+ graphemes, including one grapheme for each of the 40+ phonemes*
- read accurately by blending sounds in words with up to five known graphemes
- read some common exception words*
- read aloud books that are consistent with their phonic knowledge, without guessing words from pictures or the context of the sentence.

Language comprehension

In a familiar story/rhyme, the pupil can, when being read to by an adult (one-to-one or in a small group):
- talk about events in the story and link them to their own experiences
- retell some of the story.

Teachers should refer to the spelling appendix to the National Curriculum (English Appendix 1) to exemplify the words that pupils should be able to read as well as spell.

Standard 2 relates to any Phase 2 GPC that the child has secured. Standards 2 to 4 can be used to describe the GPCs taught in Phases 2 and 3.

Little Wandle and the Reading framework

The extract below from Section 3 of the Reading framework (2021) outlines recent research and support for the use of a systematic synthetic phonics (SSP) programme to teach reading to children with SEND. The approaches described by the Reading framework fit well with the Little Wandle approach applied within the structure of the graduated approach. The evidence in the Reading framework supports the use of an SSP to teach children with autism, with Down's Syndrome and with moderate to severe and complex needs.

Children with special educational needs and disabilities

'Schools are expected to enable access to appropriate phonics instruction for children with complex needs. Under the Equality Act 2010, they are required to make reasonable adjustments to enable pupils with disabilities to have full access to the curriculum and to be able to participate in it.

Consensus is growing among academics and teachers that the best reading instruction for children with SEND is SSP, taught by direct instruction. They can learn to read and write and can make progress towards or attain functional literacy.

In a 2021 French study of children with learning disabilities, Sermier said:

These findings suggest that students with [special educational needs] benefit from phonics-based programs integrating research-based approaches and techniques.[1]

Similarly, a recent systematic review for children with autism by Arcuili and Bailey concluded:

... comprehensive instruction that incorporates [phonemic awareness, phonics, vocabulary, reading fluency and reading comprehension] ... is not only appropriate for children with autism but also effective.[2]

The view that children learn in different ways is under scrutiny. Dehaene has said:

... it is simply not true that there are hundreds of ways to learn to read. Every child is unique... but when it comes to reading, we all have roughly the same brain that imposes the same constraints and the same learning sequence.[3]

Evidence suggests that most children with moderate to severe and complex needs are not 'visual learners', as previously thought. Trembath, for instance, in a small study, found 'no evidence of a prominent visual learning style in children with ASD,'[4] while Kathy Cologon has noted that, for children with Down's syndrome:

Sight-word learning on its own is insufficient for reading development and teaching with this approach alone is contrary to current evidence-based practices in literacy instruction.[5]

SSP, rather than a whole-word approach, provides children with moderate to severe and complex needs the best opportunity to gain functional literacy. Children who have a hearing or visual impairment are generally able to access phonics teaching if they have some hearing or vision.

Instruction should be accessible to all these children. Teachers should:
- provide them with the skills and knowledge they need to read and spell, by direct instruction, progressing systematically with carefully structured, small and cumulative steps
- use instructional routines that become familiar
- provide materials that limit distraction; are clear, linear and easy to follow; are age-neutral or age-appropriate and can be adapted further, such as being reduced to individual items
- provide opportunities for work on vocabulary, fluency and reading comprehension
- provide multiple opportunities for overlearning (recall, retrieval, practice and application at the level of the alphabetic code, word, sentence and text).

Teaching should:
- be at a suitable pace for the child because progression through a programme will be much slower than for their typically developing peers
- be daily, with well-paced, well-planned lessons that are engaging and motivating
- take full account of the child's individual strengths, weaknesses, knowledge and understanding, and profile of needs.

Some children may need additional strategies, such as for those who:
- have physical disabilities that affect their fine motor control for holding and manipulating objects, e.g. use of desktop manipulatives, alternative writing strategies
- are pre- or non-verbal, e.g. use of alternative communication strategies, such as selecting their response from auditory choices anchored to visual symbols or place-markers
- have both fine motor difficulties and are pre- or non-verbal, e.g. use of low- or high-tech eye gaze strategies.

A very few children with profound and multiple learning difficulties (PMLD) might not be able to access direct literacy instruction but might access alternative activities to teach children how letters correspond to sounds within the context of a pre-formal sensory curriculum.'

Footnotes from the Reading framework appendix:

1. Sermier D and others (2021). 'Effects of a phonics-based intervention on the reading skills of students with intellectual disability' Research in Developmental Disabilities: volume 111

2. Arcuili J and Bailey B (2021). 'The promise of comprehensive early reading instruction for children with autism and recommendations for future directions' Language, Speech and Hearing Services in Schools: volume 52, issue 1, pages 225-238

3. Dehaene S (2009). 'Reading in the Brain' London: Penguin Random House

4. Trembath D and others (2015). 'Accurate or Assumed: Visual Learning in Children with ASD' Journal of Autism and Developmental Disorders: volume 45, pages 3276-3287

5. Cologon K (2013). 'Debunking myths: Reading development in children with Down Syndrome' Australian Journal of Teacher Education: volume 38, number 3

Little Wandle and the Education Inspection Framework (EIF)

Special schools will receive the same deep dive into reading as mainstream schools and Ofsted will pay particular attention to children at Key Stage 2 who are unable to read, and the school's provision for those children. But it is important to understand how the provision in special schools is protected by the SEND Code of Practice (2014) and Equality Act (2010) to uphold the rights of the child to receive both reasonable adjustments and access to high-quality provision. The quotations in the tinted panels below are from Ofsted's *Education Inspection Framework* (EIF).

Key points to consider are that children's starting points and specific needs are individual, and this must be taken into account when planning their curriculum.

> '366. Pupils with SEND have a range of different needs and starting points. Some pupils have severe, complex or profound needs that have a significant impact on their cognitive development, especially the way that they are able to make alterations to their long-term memory. Other pupils have starting points at least as high as other pupils of their age, for instance some pupils with sensory impairments.'

Special schools need to understand how Ofsted inspects early reading according to the EIF and how these aspects of the inspection apply to each of their pupils. This includes the teaching of reading using phonics and matching children's secure phonic knowledge to the right books.

> '367. All parts of the EIF apply to state-funded and non-maintained special schools' provision and to mainstream schools' provision for pupils with SEND. However, as with all provision, SEND provision has some specific factors that should be taken into account.'

Evaluating impact

An inspection of any school will evaluate the impact of the education provided by the school. The focus will primarily be on what pupils have learned. This means that special schools using Little Wandle can show they have a well-structured progression that is cumulative and provides repetition and practice.

The assessment documents and planning documents can show progress over time – even in very small steps. Using the small-step approach and planning documents, schools can show how new learning is built upon and reinforced through repeated practice (see the Reading framework).

'221. Inspection experience and research show that the most important factors to consider are the following:

- A well-constructed, well-taught curriculum will lead to pupils learning more and so achieving good results. Therefore, such a curriculum contributes to evidence of impact. There need be no conflict between teaching a broad, rich curriculum and achieving success in examinations and tests.

- Disadvantaged pupils and pupils with SEND acquire the knowledge and cultural capital they need to succeed in life.

- Pupils are making progress in that they know more, remember more and are able to do more. They are learning what is intended in the curriculum.

- All learning builds towards an end point. Pupils are being prepared for their next stage of education, training or employment at each stage of their learning. Inspectors will consider whether pupils are ready for the next stage by the point they leave the school or provision that they attend.

- If pupils are not able to read to an age-appropriate level and fluency, they will be incapable of accessing the rest of the curriculum, and they will rapidly fall behind their peers.*'

*This only applies to 'pupils (who) have starting points at least as high as other pupils of their age.' But fluency is the aim for all pupils – that is the 'end point' we are aiming for, for all our children.

Using the assessment materials to determine the correct SEND pathway

You will need to assess all children on entry to the SEND programme so their pathway and specific teaching plan can be created. Assess all children, except those starting at the beginning of Phase 2. The SEND assessments, assessment guidance and supporting videos can be found in the SEND area of the Little Wandle website, and you will find detailed information on how to carry out the assessments there.

By using these assessments, you will be able to work out exactly what gaps these children have, and put in place the appropriate pathway and programme to ensure they learn to read. The assessments will also help you match children to the appropriate reading book.

Three potential pathways for children with SEND are set out on pages 15 to 17.

Assessment of progress

Children following **Pathway 1**, the main programme, should be assessed using the summative assessments for that programme. Their data should be uploaded onto the members' pupil analysis website (https://analysis.littlewandlelettersandsounds.org.uk).

Children following **Pathway 2** or **Pathway 3**, and who have just started the programme, should be assessed using the SEND summative assessments after five weeks of teaching. The small-step assessment spreadsheet can measure progress in oral blending, phonemic awareness, GPC knowledge, blending words to read and word reading. The assessments, advice and spreadsheet can be found in the SEND area of the Little Wandle website.

Fluency assessments

The fluency assessment should be used to find out about children's reading accuracy and rate of reading as they become more confident readers at Phase 5, and to tell you whether or not children have gained enough fluency and accuracy to exit the programme. In order to understand the meaning of what they are reading, children need to be reading at approximately 60 to 70 words per minute.

Please refer to the assessment guidance in the SEND area of the Little Wandle website to find out how to carry out initial and subsequent assessments.

Exiting the programme

Children may take a long time to secure fluent reading. It is crucial that children are taught to read until they are fully fluent and can read, using adaptive technology if needed, to the point of independence. All children need to complete the programme, secure the Phase 5 core graphemes and read words with these GPCs in them with ease. For some SEND children, reading at this speed may not be possible even though they have secured the full alphabetic code – due to their processing speeds. The decision to stop phonics instruction should be made by considering the fluency level for that child – will they be able to read with independence, can they access the wider curriculum through reading, are they secure enough to not need repeated practice any more? Children can, of course, have a refresher on any aspect of reading if needed.

Even when children are ready to stop their phonics instruction, they will need to continue the Reading practice sessions with the Phase 5 set 5 reading books for age 7+. Reading these books will ensure that they are practising their phonic knowledge in context and provide challenge in terms of vocabulary and comprehension.

Continue to use the SEND Grapheme mat for Phases 2, 3 and 5 in class to aid spelling and ensure that the children are given time to use their phonic knowledge to decode new words when they are reading.

Pathway 1

Pathway 1 is for children who are ready for phonics and can access the **main programme** with minor adaptations (for example, to meet their sensory needs). You will use the individual or group **Keep-up** materials to support these children.

> Teaching of the *Little Wandle Letters and Sounds Revised* main programme with:

Adaptations to pace as appropriate. For example, these children may cover one to three new GPCs per week, not four.	**Adaptations to resources** as appropriate. For example, these children may be supported by the use of sensory grapheme cards/large grapheme cards, word cards with larger print, or additional sensory resources used alongside the grapheme cards.

Use the Little Wandle main programme assessments (every five weeks) to assess progress and identify the individual or group keep-up needed for each child.

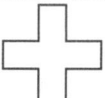

When needed, use individual or group keep-up from the Little Wandle main programme. Use the main programme assessment again after three weeks to check that the children have filled their gaps.

Timetable Reading practice sessions using decodable reading books from the Little Wandle main programme. Use the main programme assessment to match each child's secure phonic knowledge to the appropriate decodable reading book.

Pathway 2

Pathway 2 is for children who need the **graduated approach** and lessons with a lower cognitive load. Teachers can plan lessons using the **SEND weekly grids** and direct the pace of teaching to match the needs of the child/group. The SEND weekly grids should be used flexibly; the lessons can be chunked up and used over longer periods of time to match the adaptations of pace that children need.

Children should be supported by the use of: sensory grapheme cards/large grapheme cards, word cards with larger print, or additional sensory resources used alongside the grapheme cards, if needed.

At Phases 2 and 3, the first step is to teach children the GPCs for that phase in lessons focusing solely on teaching these GPCs. When they are ready, the children will then apply the GPCs they have learned in lessons that focus on blending. Oral and teacher-led blending practice continues throughout Phases 4 and 5.

At Phase 5, you should continue to teach GPCs before moving on to the words and activities in the weekly grids. Each GPC is introduced with an example word and image, for example 'ou' /ow/ 'cloud'. Use the SEND Phase 5 grapheme cards to support teaching.

> Teach GPCs and tricky words following the graduated approach as outlined on pages 30 to 31.

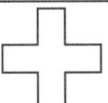

> Use oral blending games from the Little Wandle SEND programme. Refer to the blending **Prompt cards** (pages 32 to 55) and 'How to' videos to support your teaching.

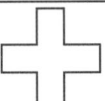

> Teach blending and reading using the appropriate SEND weekly grids and assess every five weeks. Refer to the blending **Prompt cards** (pages 32 to 55) and 'How to' videos to support your teaching. Use the super-supported, supported and whisper methods for teacher-led blending flexibly to meet the child's needs.

> Use the Little Wandle SEND programme assessments (every five weeks) to record children's progress and plan next steps for teaching using the 'Individual progress' document.

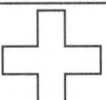

> Teach Reading practice sessions using the blending practice books and decodable reading books. The SEND programme assessment will help you match the child's secure phonic knowledge to the appropriate decodable reading book.

Pathway 3

Pathway 3 is for children who need the **graduated approach** to teach all or most aspects of the programme. They might be starting with pre-phonics using the SEND Foundations for phonics activities (in the SEND area of the Little Wandle website) and then move on to phonics and reading instruction using the graduated approach.

This pathway will ensure a smaller-step progression to the point of challenge for that child. To create this pathway, teachers will use the **Prompt cards** (pages 32 to 55), the **SEND programme progression** (pages 18 to 21) and adapt the SEND weekly grids (in the SEND area of the Little Wandle website) where necessary.

Children should be supported by the use of additional sensory resources, if needed.

Teaching of pre-phonics. Use the 'How to' videos for
SEND Foundations for phonics to support your delivery.

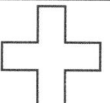

Use oral blending games from the Little Wandle SEND programme. Refer to the blending **Prompt cards** (pages 32 to 55) and 'How to' videos to support your teaching. .

When ready for the graduated approach of the SEND programme,
use the Little Wandle SEND programme assessments (every five weeks)
to identify the next steps for teaching Phase 2.

Little Wandle SEND programme progression

This programme overview shows the progression of GPCs and tricky words that we teach, in order. The progression has been organised so that children are taught from the simple to more complex GPCs, as well as taking into account the frequency of their occurrence in the most commonly encountered words. All the graphemes taught are practised in words, sentences and, later on, in fully decodable books. Children review and revise GPCs and words daily, weekly and across terms and years, in order to move this knowledge into their long-term memory.

Phase 2

Graphemes	Coverage in Phase 2 weekly grids (Words should be introduced only when focus GPCs are secure)						
s a t	Week 1	Week 2	Week 3	Week 4	Week 5	Week 6	Week 7
p i n							
m d							
g o c							
k ck							
e u							
r h							
b f							
l ll							
ff ss							
j v							
w x y							
z zz							
qu th							
ch sh							
ng nk							
Tricky words*	I is the	put* pull* full*	as and has	his her go	no to into	she push* of	he we me be

Phase 3

Graphemes	Coverage in Phase 3 weekly grids (Words should be introduced only when focus GPCs are secure)				
Review Phase 2 GPCs	Week 1	Week 2	Week 3	Week 4	Week 5
ai ee					
igh oa					
oo **oo**					
ar or					
ur ow					
oi ear					
air er					
Tricky words (review)*	I is the put* pull*	full* as and has his	her go no to into	she push* he of we	me be

*Tricky words are included on the weekly grids for convenience but should be taught outside of the blending practice sessions in Phases 2 and 3. The words 'put', 'pull', 'full' and 'push' are not tricky in some regional pronunciations, in which case they should not be treated as such. They can be taught in teacher-led blending.

Phase 4

Focus word type	Example words	Taught in weekly grids
Adjacent consonants with short vowels		
CVCC	hand	Week 1
CCVC	spot	Week 2
CCVCC	stamp	Week 3
CCCVC	string	Week 4
CCCVCC	strict	
Adjacent consonants with long vowels		
CVCC	paint	Week 5
CCVC, CCV	green, star	Week 6
CCVCC, CCCVC	spoilt, sprain	Week 7
Adjacent consonants with short vowels and suffixes		
–ing	resting	Week 7
–er	swimmer	
–est	longest	
–ed /id/	landed	
–ed /t/	dressed	Week 8
Adjacent consonants with long vowels and suffixes		
–ing	painting	Week 8
–er	toaster	
–est	smartest	
–ed /id/	painted	
–ed /d/	groaned	Week 10
Two-syllable words		
With short vowels	plastic	Week 9
With long vowels	frighten	Week 10

Tricky words (new words in bold)	**Weeks revised/taught**
the I no go to	Week 1
into we me be of	Week 2
was you they my all	Week 3
are sure come do have	Week 4
here like little love one	Week 5
out said says some so	Week 6
there today were what when	Week 7
put pull full push he	Week 8
she **by pure** come do	Week 9
have here like little love	Week 10

Phase 5

Not all Phase 5 graphemes from the main Little Wandle programme are taught in the Phase 5 SEND weekly grids. The 40 most common and useful GPCs are taught – these are the Phase 5 core graphemes. Some GPCs are taught as variants in words only, for example, /j/ 'ge' as in 'fringe' and /s/ 'ce' as in 'fence'.

These Phase 5 core graphemes will give children enough understanding of Phase 5 to be able to decode most common words whilst keeping the number of graphemes small enough to be manageable. Each Phase 5 core grapheme card has an image on it to help create a strong link; these are replicated in the SEND Grapheme mat for Phases 2, 3 and 5.

Graphemes	Example word	Taught in weekly grid
/ai/ ay	crayons	Week 1
/ow/ ou	cloud	
/oi/ oy	toy	
/ee/ ea	beach	Week 2
/ur/ ir	bird	
/igh/ ie	pie	
/oo/ ue	blue	Week 3
/yoo/ ue	statue	
/yoo/ u	unicorn	
/oa/ o	robot	Week 4
/igh/ i	spider	
/ai/ a	apron	
/ee/ e	lemur	Week 5
/oa/ ow	rainbow	
/ai/ a-e	cake	
/igh/ i-e	bike	Week 6
/oa/ o-e	fishbone	
/oo/ /yoo/ u-e	tubes/cute	
/ee/ e-e	athlete	Week 7
/oo/ /yoo/ ew	jewels/new	

Graphemes	Example word	Taught in weekly grid
/ee/ ie	shield	Week 8
/or/ aw	paws	
/ee/ y	jelly	
/e/ ea	bread	Week 9
/w/ wh	wheel	
/igh/ y	butterfly	
/j/ g	giant	Week 10
/j/ dge (ge)	bridge (fringe)	
/s/ c (ce)	mice (fence)	
/f/ ph	elephant	
/air/ are	square	Week 11
/z/ se	cheese	
/l/ le	apple	
/v/ ve	leaves	Week 12
/u/ o	gloves	
/o/ a	watch	
/or/ a (al)	ball (walk)	Week 13
/sh/ ti	station	
/sh/ ci	magician	
/or/ ore	before	Week 14

The graphemes in brackets are taught in Phase 5 as variants in words; 'tch' is also taught as a variant of /ch/.

Tricky words (new words in bold)	Weeks revised/ taught
said says so some there	Week 1
today were what when come	Week 2
do have here like little	Week 3
love one **our their people**	Week 4
oh your Mr Mrs Ms	Week 5
ask* could would should our	Week 6
house mouse water want any	Week 7

Tricky words (new words in bold)	Weeks revised/ taught
many again who whole where	Week 8
two school call different thought	Week 9
through friend work once laugh	Week 10
because eye busy beautiful pretty	Week 11
house **move improve parents shoe**	Week 12
their people oh your Mr	Week 13
Mrs Ms ask could our	Week 14

*The word 'ask' is not tricky in some regional pronunciations, in which case it should not be treated as such.

Teaching Little Wandle SEND

We have provided a range of resources to support teachers with the planning and delivery of phonics lessons and Reading practice sessions. Use the resources flexibly in your teaching to match the needs of each child. Always teach to the point of challenge – we can have high expectations for every child if we put the correct adaptations, support and repeated practice in place.

Timetabling phonics lessons and Reading practice sessions

Timetabling will depend on the specific needs of the children and on staff resourcing. Phonics lessons should be timetabled daily, if possible, and the teaching and practice of GPCs and words should continue until they are secure.

You will also need to timetable Reading practice sessions – ideally three a week. These sessions are essential so that children have quality teaching of reading and time to apply their secure phonic knowledge in age-appropriate decodable books. Children need to read each decodable book three times, and books should only be taken home for further reading practice after the final read.

Typically, you will be teaching individuals or small groups. The phonics lessons and Reading practice sessions can be used for small groups if the children have been assessed to have largely the same needs. You could also consider mixed year groups. All of the resources and activities in this guide can be used with individuals or groups of children.

Phonics lessons

Teaching GPCs
Teach GPCs **before** children encounter them in the words and activities in the SEND weekly grids. Use the Prompt cards on pages 33 to 39 and the 'How to' videos on the website for guidance on how to teach GPCs. Once the children have secured enough GPCs to start learning to blend, use the Phase 2 and 3 blending practice templates on pages 56 to 57 and the weekly grids to teach and practise this skill. Blending is key at Phase 4 so do not progress to Phase 4 until children understand how to blend, either orally or in their heads. At Phase 5, you should continue to teach GPCs before moving on to the words and activities in the weekly grids, but each GPC is introduced with an example word, such as 'ou' /ow/ 'cloud'. Use the SEND Phase 5 grapheme cards to teach Phase 5 GPCs.

Teaching blending
Concentrate on teaching Phase 2/3 GPCs for a number of weeks and then move on to applying them through teaching blending, using the words in the Phase 2 and 3 weekly grids. You can then return to teaching more GPCs and repeat the cycle.

The blending practice lessons, outlined in the templates on pages 56 to 57, form the basis of teaching blending and are for children who can read some GPCs but cannot blend – yet! They should be run by a trained teacher or teaching assistant and focus solely on blending using GPCs that the children know – first orally, and then with graphemes.

There are seven weeks of daily blending practice lessons for Phase 2 and five for Phase 3, and they build cumulatively. Children who complete all the lessons should be able to read words with all the Phase 2 and 3 GPCs. However, you can use the lessons for as long as needed, and they can be repeated and broken down into smaller chunks to suit the needs of your children.

You will find detailed guidance on the different methods used in teaching blending in the Prompt cards on pages 40 to 45. Children need to learn how to blend before starting Phase 4 but blending practice continues throughout the Little Wandle SEND programme and is covered on the weekly grids for all phases.

Teaching tricky words

Tricky words are introduced in Phase 2 in Little Wandle SEND, as in the main programme, and are included in the weekly grids for convenience. However, you should teach tricky words in Phases 2 and 3 outside of the blending practice lessons detailed in the templates (pages 56 to 57).

Use the Prompt card on page 46 for guidance on teaching tricky words. Tricky words are also included in the spelling activities in Phases 4 and 5 (see page 52). In Phases 4 and 5, tricky words can be taught in phonics lessons or separately to suit the child's needs.

Using the weekly grids

Use the weekly grids flexibly. Each lesson can be chunked up and taught over a number of sessions and it can be revisited as many times as needed. Optional phrases and sentences to read have been included for each phase, but they need not be taught within the lesson, and they can be used later to increase challenge. As described above, you may wish to concentrate on teaching several GPCs for a number of weeks and before teaching blending, reading and spelling using the weekly grids.

Reading practice sessions

Match books to children's secure phonic knowledge

Use the assessments to work out which books match the children's secure phonic knowledge. The SEND assessment spreadsheet will give you the best match for each child, but you should use your professional judgement as well. If a book level seems too difficult or easy, try the level above or below to see if it is a better fit.

If children are making quicker progress in between assessments, you can also use your judgement to move them on to the next level of book. Check the child can read:

- the GPCs in the book effortlessly

- the practice words at the front of the book fluently (with little or no overt blending)

- the tricky words.

Now ask them to read the first double-page spread. Can they read it without hesitation? If so, then this is the correct level.

Adapting the three reads

Children need to be given regular opportunities to apply the phonics they have learned to reading fully decodable books. The phonic progression in these books must match the progression of *Little Wandle Letters and Sounds Revised*. Reading practice sessions should take place at least three times a week. Each Reading practice session needs to have a clear focus, so that the demands of the session do not overload the children's working memory.

The Reading practice sessions have been designed to focus on three key reading skills:

* decoding

* prosody – reading with meaning, stress and intonation

* comprehension – understanding the text.

For some SEND children, the three reads may take longer. Reading practice sessions can be adapted and taught to meet the needs of individuals or groups. A book can be taught over two weeks rather than one. Sensory elements, pictures and other adaptations can be added to ensure children make strong connections between the book and their knowledge of the world. This will enable them to read the book with the greatest level of success possible.

The **decoding** session might be repeated to aid fluency, or the book might be chunked up to two sessions, depending on the needs of the child.

Teaching **prosody** is an important skill for all children. Some children with an autistic spectrum condition (ASC), auditory processing disorder or hearing impairment may not be able to produce prosody when speaking. However, talking through how and why specific emphasis carries meaning beyond the words themselves is helpful in teaching how spoken prosody affects comprehension.

Teach **comprehension** through talk and by making connections between the book and the children's lives. Dialogic talk is the best way to grow vocabulary and language. When children make connections between books and their interests, they are growing their foundational knowledge of reading and finding out how it will benefit them and give them pleasure.

Using the blending practice books

The Little Wandle blending practice books all focus on specific Phase 2 and Phase 3 GPCs. They are much shorter in length, have sound buttons beneath the words and have been designed so that children can practise their blending skills in context. The books are richly illustrated and provide lots of opportunity to extend language and comprehension.

Children read the words or phrases on each double-page spread and then find the corresponding object, animal or person in the illustrations. When they turn over to the next double-page spread, they will find out if they were correct.

Phase 2: The Phase 2 blending practice books for the main programme cover the GPCs in small steps and are ideal for children who find the step up to reading the Phase 2 decodable books too much.

Phase 3: The Phase 3 blending practice books for the main programme cover specific Phase 3 GPCs in each book. These books may well meet the needs of many children who find the main programme books too long and complex.

Blending practice books for age 7+: The 7+ blending practice books cover Phases 2 and 3 in larger chunks and are more challenging than the blending books for the main programme. They are also designed to appeal to slightly older children in terms of content and interest level.

All of these books can be read using the three reads model, support for which can be found in the SEND area of the Little Wandle website. They can be used flexibly to meet the needs of each child and provide practice for blending in context.

Which books?

All the Big Cat for Little Wandle books follow the *Little Wandle Letters and Sounds Revised* progression. You can choose the decodable books, the blending practice books or the 7+ books that best suit your learners' needs and interests. Older SEND children may prefer the content and look of the 7+ books.

Phase 5 core graphemes

Not all Phase 5 graphemes from the main programme are taught in the Phase 5 SEND weekly grids – only the most common and useful GPCs are taught. Children following the Phase 5 SEND programme can still read the Phase 5 books, but some words in these books will need to be taught to the children as tricky words before they read the book. Support for this can be found in the matching grid for SEND, which can be found in the SEND assessment guidance on the Little Wandle website.

More planning and adaptation advice for teaching reading using the Big Cat for Little Wandle books can be found on the Little Wandle website.

How to use the resources

The physical teaching resources for Little Wandle SEND have been carefully created to help you teach with fidelity to the programme and to ensure all children get the additional practice that they need to secure fluent reading of GPCs and words.

Grapheme cards

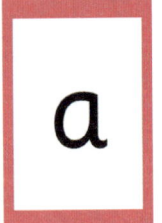     

tail in the rain   crayons

Use the **Grapheme cards**:

- To teach each new GPC in Phases 2, 3 and 5. The Phase 2, 3 and 5 grapheme cards are ideal to use when you are making the link between the grapheme, phoneme and the mnemonic/catchphrase/Phase 5 word. You may wish to use the large sensory grapheme cards for each phase. These are embossed so that children can feel the shape of the grapheme.

- To make the words used in oral and teacher-led blending. This is a crucial part of our pedagogy and ensures that children are taught to blend step by step. In this way, we model how to blend in every lesson, until the children are secure and do not need this support any more. You can see this in practice in the SEND 'How to' video 'Teacher-led blending'.

Revisit and review		Teach and practise		Practise and apply		
Oral blending games	GPCs	Oral blending	Teacher-led blending words Independent reading	Tricky words	Spelling	Reading practice sessions with blending books or decodable books three times
Can you do the actions? n-o-d your head c-l-a-p your hands t-a-p your foot r-u-b your tummy	l o g ck u b i r a t e d	l-o-g l-o-ck l-u-ck	Teacher-led: **log lock luck red** Independent: **big rat**	his	big rat	
Blend from the box f-r-o-g f-i-sh h-a-t c-r-ow-n	b e ll t i s a o p d	b-e-ll t-e-ll b-i-ll	Teacher-led: **bell tell bill bed** Independent: **sat top**		sat top	
Can you touch your … ? l-e-g ch-ee-k b-a-ck h-ee-l	o ff h u p c a t	o-ff h-u-ff	Teacher-led: **off huff puff cat** Independent: **cup hat**	her	cup hat	
Point to the …	m e ss h i f u t n				ten man	

Use the grapheme cards for teacher-led blending

- When reviewing GPCs. Remember to use the grapheme side; only use the mnemonic/catchphrase/Phase 5 word if the children cannot automatically read the grapheme.

- For **Change it**. This game is part of the lessons in Phases 4 and 5. You can see it in practice in the 'How to' video 'Change it'.

- For **Mix it up**. Use the small grapheme cards to model spelling and for children to spell words in this one-to-one activity. You can see the activity in practice in the 'How to' video 'Mix it up'.

Tip: A pocket chart or stand is very useful. Make sure you have all your graphemes in order, so you can make the changes easily!

Picture cards

Use the **Picture cards** when introducing a new GPC at Phase 2. The picture card is the same image as the mnemonic, to maximise on the link between the phoneme, mnemonic, and the grapheme.

Word cards

There are three sets of word cards for Little Wandle SEND:

Blending cards: for use in blending practice sessions at Phases 2 and 3 (for independent reading only – use grapheme cards to make the words for teacher-led blending).

Word cards for independent reading at Phases 3, 4 and 5.

Tricky word cards for all phases.

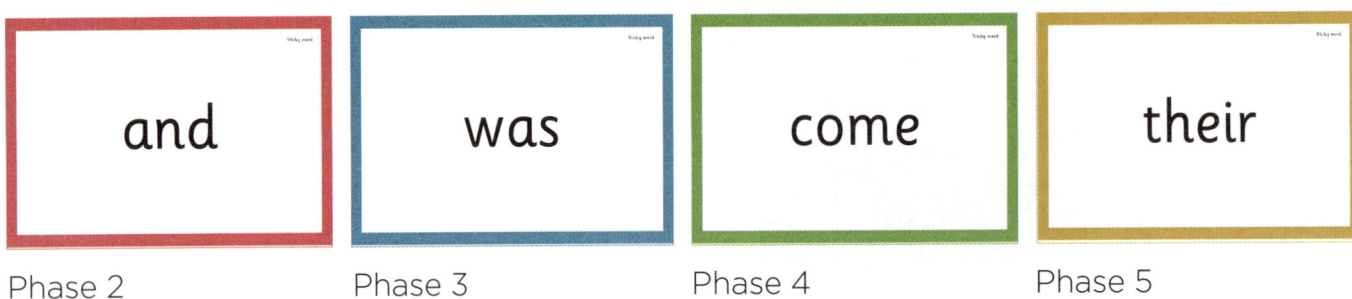

Phase 2   Phase 3   Phase 4   Phase 5

The word cards have coloured borders to indicate their phase, and a label in the top right-hand corner to indicate their use. Blending cards and word cards are double sided, with sound buttons on one side and just the word on the other. Tricky word cards are single sided and do not have sound buttons.

Organising your word cards

Multiple copies of words needed for review are provided so that you can organise your cards into sets according to the weekly grids. However, there is just one copy of each tricky word, and we recommend you organise these alphabetically so that you can find them quickly when needed for review.

> **Tip:** The words from the previous week(s) can stay in your pocket chart so they are easy to find and review in your lesson or at any other time.

How we chose the words

There are approximately 700 words and tricky words taught in the SEND programme. These are made up of the words we orally blend; words we make using grapheme cards in teacher-led blending; and the words on the word cards and tricky word cards.

Decodable words

We chose the words for the SEND programme carefully, by using the original research from the 2007 *Letters and Sounds*[1], which identified the 300 most common words, and the Collins Corpus, which extracted the most frequent words from 1.2 million words in 950 titles aimed at children aged three to 11. In this way, we could teach children to read words that would have the greatest impact on their reading as efficiently as possible. We have organised these words into a cumulative progression.

Tricky words

The tricky words remain the same as those in the main Little Wandle programme. They are the original tricky words from *Letters and Sounds* (2007) combined with the Common Exception Words from the English National Curriculum Year 1 and 2 Spelling appendix.

[1] *Masterson, J., Stuart, M., Dixon, M. and Lovejoy, S. (2003) Children's Printed Word Database: Economic and Social Research Council funded project, R00023406*

Grapheme mats

 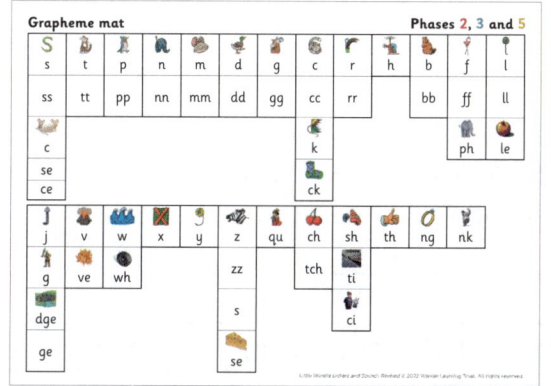

Download the grapheme mats to use with children in the lessons. There are two versions of the grapheme mat suitable for children following the SEND programme: one includes the Phase 2 and 3 graphemes only; the other also includes the Phase 5 core graphemes for SEND. Sets of laminated desktop grapheme mats are also available from Collins.

Image bank

The Little Wandle SEND images can be used to support children who are non-verbal or who need additional language support. We have provided images for as many of the words featured in the weekly grids as possible, and these can be downloaded from the SEND area of the Little Wandle website. The words that have a matching image are in **bold** in the weekly grids. Each weekly grid has a corresponding PDF download containing all the images for the week. If you need images for teaching using the graduated approach, use the image search tool in the SEND area of the website.

Fully decodable books

Alongside 204 fully decodable books for the main programme, Collins has created 50 fully decodable books for children age 7+. All the books provide practice at the correct level for each phase, as well as ensuring that children's vocabulary and language development is supported. The 7+ books may be more appropriate for your older learners.

The matching grid in the SEND assessment guidance, which can be found on the Little Wandle website, should be used to match each child's secure phonic knowledge in reading to the appropriate decodable reading books.

Blending practice books

There are 20 blending practice books for Phases 2 and 3. These books have a very limited number of words and practise specific GPCs. They are used to focus on blending skills and extending vocabulary. There are supporting teacher's notes to guide you through how to use them. You can also see these books being used in the 'How to' video 'Blending practice books'.

Using the graduated approach with Little Wandle

The graduated approach to teaching children to the point of challenge is outlined in the SEND Code of Practice (2014). This section outlines how you can use the graduated approach within the Little Wandle pedagogy.

The graduated approach	
Assess	• Work out which stage and GPC is appropriate for the child, using our assessments (the placement assessment or appropriate SEND assessments).
Plan	• Use the weekly grids to identify which GPCs and skills you are going to teach. • Plan the steps and adjustments needed to successfully teach these. • Give a clear timescale for this/decide when to review progress towards these steps.
Do	• Teach and keep notes as needed for additional adjustments, successes and extra steps needed. • From the activities described in the Prompt cards for teaching a new GPC (pages 33 to 34), choose to start with either **What's in the box?** or **Teach a new phoneme**.
Review	• Ensure regular review occurs. Consider reteaching, where more input and practice is needed.

Using the graduated approach to teach blending

Reducing cognitive load
It is important to factor in the impact of cognitive load on children. In phonics lessons, be mindful of the impact on cognitive load of the following:

The teaching environment
• Keep the visual environment clear and uncluttered – remove visual distractions.

• Keep teaching surfaces clear and easy to use.

• Put away any grapheme cards or word cards if they are not needed.

The way information is presented
• Think about how you can adapt lessons to cater to the children's working memory.

• Present new information using a combination of visual and auditory materials; the children will be less likely to experience cognitive overload as the content will be spread between the channels (audio/visual).

- Only present the children with essential information, to ensure that non-essential information does not take up some of their working memory's capacity. Do not include unnecessary details, such as anecdotes or animations.

- Consider how you can support the children when cognitive load is high for them; for example, when they need to hold more than one concept in their minds.

Teacher-modelling and language
- Teach essential information one step at a time.

- Use teacher modelling and the **copy me method** to ensure children have worked examples to learn new content or skills.

- Consider the language level of instruction and materials. Language comprehension requires working memory, and many children with SEND will have both limited working memory capacity and delayed or disordered receptive language. This makes it all the more important to minimise unnecessary language, which increases the cognitive load. Keep language simple, clear and to the point, to offer children with SEND the maximum opportunity to process and understand it and, therefore, to learn.

Adaptations for sensory input
- Place the grapheme cards in a protective plastic sleeve so the children can discover the graphemes in sensory materials.

- Use mirrors to help the children see how they make the sound.

- Use balloons and other objects that give feedback to help the children feel the sound.

- Use objects that give a sensory input. Provide visual aids where possible, for example, when blending c-a-t, have a toy cat. This aids learning and recall.

Prompt cards and 'How to' videos

Each Prompt card has an accompanying 'How to' video, which you will find in the SEND area of the Little Wandle website. Together, they show how Little Wandle can be taught using the graduated approach.

Teaching new GPCs

Blending and reading words

Practise and apply

You will find Prompt cards for Reading practice sessions in the SEND area of the Little Wandle website.

32 |

Teaching new GPCs

Phases 2 and 3: Teaching a new GPC

You will need:
- the grapheme card and picture card for the GPC you are teaching
- objects and pictures for **What's in the box?** (you can find a full list of items needed for this activity in the Phase 2 grapheme chart on pages 62 to 64)
- grapheme cards that the child can read with confidence for **Win it!**
- a sticker on which to write the grapheme for the child after the session.

What's in the box? (Phase 2)

What to do	Appropriate adjustments	Notes
• Explain that all the objects in your box begin/end with the same sound. • Take out each object, one by one. Say what it is, emphasising the initial/end sound. • Use the **copy me method** so the child says the sound and then the name of the object.	• Use objects that give a sensory input. Allow the child to feel or hold the object if appropriate. • Start with a small number of objects, which you can increase if appropriate. • Use appropriate images from the Little Wandle SEND image banks/eye gaze software/PECS. • The child may not be able to produce accurate sounds/words themselves. This does not mean that they have not understood the activity. **Pace** • This activity may need to be repeated several times, to help the child hear the phoneme and the sound in the word. • You can choose to move on to another phoneme and objects and then return to the previous phoneme and objects.	• Try to ensure the objects are within the child's vocabulary knowledge. If not, take time to explore the object and its meaning with the child. • Use objects or pictures that are of interest to the child. • The child may not be able to produce accurate sounds themselves: accept the sound they produce. • Use the Phase 2 picture card for the GPC you are teaching. • You will need to source the other objects listed in the Phase 2 grapheme chart (see page 62) for the grapheme you are teaching – the items can be amended to suit the age/interest of the child.

Teach a new phoneme

What to do	Appropriate adjustments	Notes
• Model the correct enunciation of the phoneme a few times. • Ensure the child can see how you make the sound. They need to see your mouth. • Practise saying the sound together. Then ask the child to say it after you, several times.	• Use mirrors to help the child see how they make the sound. • Use balloons and other objects that give feedback to help the child feel the sound.	• The child may not be able to produce accurate sounds: accept the sound they produce. • Prior to teaching, ensure you practise the pronunciation phrase (see the grapheme charts on pages 62 to 66) so you can teach the child how to form the phoneme correctly. • Ensure you use a clear voice, and that the child can see your mouth clearly • You may need to exaggerate your mouth movements to help the child really 'see' how to make the sound.

Teach a new grapheme

What to do	Appropriate adjustments	Notes
Step 1 • Place the picture card next to the mnemonic side of the grapheme card, so the child can see both of them. • Point to the picture and say what it is, emphasising the initial/end sound (e.g. d d d duck). • Point to the mnemonic to show that it's the same object (duck). • Repeat a few times together. **Step 2** • Draw the letter formation over the picture as you say the sound – saying the mnemonic at the end of the letter (e.g. d d d duck). • Repeat a few times, using the **copy me method**. The child can draw the letter formation over the picture as you say the sound together. **Step 3** • Show the child the grapheme side of the card. Draw the letter formation over the grapheme as you say the sound. • Repeat a few times, using the **copy me method**. • The child can draw the letter formation over the grapheme as you say the sound together. **Step 4** • Play the **Grapheme game**. Show alternate sides of the card as the child calls out. Repeat. • Always say the sound when you say the mnemonic. • Ensure there is lots of repetition of reading and saying the grapheme.	**Steps 2 and 3** • Give the child their own version of the cards, at an appropriate size, and adapt the cards to suit the child's sensory needs. • Either use the sensory grapheme cards or create sensory input by adding Wikki Stix or other materials over the grapheme so the child can trace over it. • Use other sensory inputs to explore the letter shape, e.g. roll and write alphabets, sandpaper, tactile print. • Use foam, sand, paint or other sensory items to connect with the grapheme. • Place the grapheme card in a protective plastic sleeve so the child can discover it in sensory materials. **Step 4** • Give the child the appropriate picture card/grapheme for the **Grapheme game** to point to, if they cannot produce speech sounds.	• This activity has been broken up into several small steps that can happen in one lesson or over several lessons. • Keep all sessions short and successful. **Steps 1 to 3** • These can take as many sessions as needed and may involve going backwards and forwards over the steps. **Step 4** • Play the **Grapheme game** (Step 4) lots of times to ensure the child has plenty of practice. This will help move the grapheme into their long-term memory. • The child may not be able to produce accurate sounds themselves: accept how they say the sound. • Play for as long as the child enjoys this game and stop whilst the child is successful. • Write the new grapheme on a sticker and stick it on the child's top or sleeve in such a way that they can look down and read it. • Make sure the class teacher and parent/carer are told which grapheme the child is learning with you, so they can practise it with the child at other times.
Win it! (one-to-one lessons only) • Add the new grapheme card to the review pack. Make sure it is close to the top of the pack. • Each time the child reads the new grapheme correctly, the game stops and they 'win' the card. • Ask the child to give you the card back to see if they can win it again. • Shuffle and repeat, incrementally moving the new card back.	• Have a separate set of grapheme cards placed in front of the child so they can point to the correct grapheme as they say the sound. • The child may not be able to produce accurate sounds themselves: accept how they say the sound.	• Choose graphemes that the child can read securely for **Win it!** • If they do not read a grapheme easily, put that grapheme to the side and teach it in the next session. • Play **Win it!** a few times, putting the new grapheme back several cards each time, to ensure the child has lots of practice. This will help move the grapheme into their long-term memory.

Phases 2 and 3: Teaching a digraph/trigraph

You will need:

- the grapheme card for the Phase 2 or 3 GPC you are teaching
- grapheme cards that the child can read with confidence for **Win it!**
- a sticker on which to write the grapheme for the child after the session.

What to do	Appropriate adjustments	Notes
Phoneme		
• Model the correct enunciation of the phoneme a few times. • Ensure the child can see how you make the sound. • Practise saying the sound together. Then ask the child to say it after you, several times.	• Use a mirror to help the child see how they make the sound. • Use balloons and other objects that give feedback, to help the child feel the sound. • If the child cannot produce accurate speech sounds, accept the sounds they can make.	• The Phase 2 digraphs (excluding double letters) are 'ck', 'qu', 'th', 'ch' 'sh', 'ng' and 'nk'. • Ensure you use a clear voice. • Remind the child that the Phase 3 graphemes 'igh', 'ear' and 'air' are trigraphs – *'three letters, one sound'*. • Always say the sound when you say the catchphrase, including in the **copy me method** and **Grapheme game**. • Use a variety of 'voices' to say the catchphrase – high, low, loud, whisper, etc. The catchphrase is the 'hook' to help the child remember the grapheme – make sure it sticks!
Grapheme		
• Show the child the mnemonic/catchphrase side of the grapheme card, making a connection between the image, the sound and the catchphrase. • Teach the catchphrase. • Repeat a few times, using the **copy me method**. • Use the digraph mantra *'two letters, one sound'* (*'three letters, one sound'* for trigraphs). • Show the child the grapheme side of the card as you say the sound. • Draw the letter formation over the grapheme as you say the sound. • Repeat a few times, using the **copy me method**. The child can draw the letter formation over the picture as you say the sound together. • Remind the child of the catchphrase. • Play the **Grapheme game**. Show alternate sides of the card as the child calls out. Repeat.	• Give the child their own version of the grapheme card, at an appropriate size, and adapt the card to suit the child's sensory needs. • Either use the sensory grapheme cards or create sensory input by adding textured materials, such as Wikki Stix, over the grapheme so the child can trace over it. • Give the child the appropriate picture card/grapheme to point to in the **Grapheme game** and **Win it!**, if they cannot produce speech sounds.	• Write the new grapheme on a sticker and stick it on the child's top or sleeve in such a way that they can look down and read it. • Make sure the class teacher and parent/carer are told which graphemes the child is learning with you, so they can practise them with the child at other times
Win it! • If you are working with an individual child, play **Win it!** (page 34).		

Phase 5: Teaching a new GPC and reading a word

You will need:

- the grapheme card for the GPC you are teaching
- the SEND Grapheme mat for Phases 2, 3 and 5
- grapheme cards that the child can read with confidence for **Grapheme spotter** and **Win it!**
- the word card to match the grapheme card – use the sound button side
- a sticker on which to write the grapheme for the child after the session.

Note: Break up this lesson into smaller chunks if necessary.

What to do	Appropriate adjustments	Notes
Phoneme		
• Introduce the new phoneme. • Model the correct enunciation a few times. Ensure the child can see how you make the sound. • Use the **copy me method** to get the child to practise saying the sound after you, several times.	• Use a mirror to help the child see how they make the sound. • Use balloons and other objects that give feedback, to help the child feel the sound. • If the child cannot produce accurate speech sounds, accept the sounds they can make.	• Ensure you use a clear voice and make sure the child can see your mouth. • Take note of all previous linked graphemes, which can be found on the SEND Grapheme mat for Phases 2, 3 and 5. There may be more than one.
Grapheme		
• Show the picture side of the card, point and say what it is, emphasising the sound (e.g. ai ai ai cake). • Point to the image and say what it is, 'cake', followed by the phoneme /ai/. • Repeat a few times, using the **copy me method**. • Show the child the grapheme side of the card as you say the sound. If it is a digraph or trigraph, use the mantra 'two/three letters, one sound'. • Draw the letter formation over the grapheme as you say the sound. • Repeat a few times, using the **copy me method**. The child can trace the letter formation as you say the sound together. • Ask the child to read the grapheme as you hide it and then show it, several times. • Add the new grapheme card to the review pack. • Play **Grapheme spotter** with the new GPC. • Play **Win it!** (one-to-one lessons only; see page 34).	• Give the child their own version of the grapheme card, at an appropriate size, and adapt the card to suit the child's sensory needs. • Either use the sensory grapheme cards or create sensory input by adding textured materials, such as Wikki Stix, over the grapheme so the child can trace over it. • Give the child the appropriate picture card/grapheme to point to in the **Grapheme spotter** game, if they cannot produce speech sounds.	• Make a sticker with the new grapheme written on it, and stick it on the child's top or sleeve so they can look down and read it later. • Make sure the class teacher and parent/carer are told which graphemes the child is learning with you so that they can practise them with the child at other times.

Grow the code

• Show the child the grapheme cards for the previously taught graphemes for the new sound. • Point to the new grapheme on the SEND Grapheme mat for Phases 2, 3 and 5. Ask the child to point to the other linked graphemes that they know.	• Provide grapheme cards for the previously taught graphemes for the new focus sounds, rather than asking the child to identify the previously taught graphemes on the grapheme mat, if that will be more achievable for them.	

Read the word

Child		
• Use the word card that matches the word on the grapheme card. • Put the word card with the new grapheme in front of the child. Use the sound button side. • Ask if they can point to the new grapheme in the word. If it is a digraph or trigraph, use the mantra *'two/three letters, one sound'*. • Ask the child to sound-talk each grapheme and then blend to read the word aloud. • Ask them to point to each grapheme and then sweep beneath as they blend. If the child is not successful, do it together then ask them to try again alone. **Together** • Ask the child to join in and point to each grapheme, then say its phoneme together, sweep and blend the word. This aids fluency and helps the child hear the word pronounced correctly. • Repeat several times: the child reading alone and then together.	• Use objects that give a sensory input. Provide visual aids where possible: when blending 'snake', have a toy snake. This aids learning and recall. • Use enlarged word cards if needed. • The child may not be able to produce accurate sounds/words themselves; accept the sounds they make. • Ensure that the child knows the meaning of each word. Model how to use the word in a sentence if it is unfamiliar. • Return to blending using the whisper method (see page 44) if the child is struggling to sound out and blend the words independently. • Metacognition can help children learn. Remind the child how they blend to read words. Ask them to think about how they sound out each sound and then blend the sounds together to read the word.	• As the child sound-talks the word, nod your head to prompt them with the number of sounds.

Phase 5: Teaching graphemes that have more than one sound, e.g. 'ow' /ow/ /oa/

You will need:
- the Phase 3 grapheme card that has the same sound as the Phase 5 GPC you are teaching (e.g. 'ow' /ow/ 'wow owl')
- the Phase 5 grapheme card (e.g. 'ow' /oa/ 'rainbow')
- grapheme cards that the child can read with confidence for **Win it!**
- a sticker on which to write the grapheme for the child after the session.

What to do	Appropriate adjustments	Notes
Phoneme		
• Model the correct enunciation of the phoneme a few times. • Ensure the child can see how you make the sound. • Practise saying the sound together. • Then ask the child to say it after you, several times.	• Use enlarged grapheme cards if needed. • Use a mirror to help the child see how they make the sound. • Use balloons and other objects that give feedback, to help the child feel the sound. • If the child cannot produce accurate speech sounds, accept the sounds they can make.	• Ensure you use a clear voice, and that the child can see your mouth as you model how to say the phoneme.
Compare the phonemes		
• Show the Phase 5 grapheme card (grapheme side). Explain that they have met this grapheme before, and that it makes more than one sound. • Show the card for the grapheme that they've met before (picture side). • Point to the picture and say the catchphrase, e.g. 'wow owl'. • Point to the new picture and say the word, e.g. 'rainbow'. Repeat several times so the child can really hear the two different phonemes. • Tell the child to say the correct sound as you point to each picture.	• Give the child their own version of the grapheme card, at an appropriate size, and adapt the card to suit the child's sensory needs. • Either use the sensory grapheme cards or create sensory input by adding textured materials, such as Wikki Stix, over the grapheme so the child can trace over it. • Give the child the appropriate picture card/grapheme to point to in the **Grapheme spotter** game, if they cannot produce speech sounds.	• Phase 5 core graphemes that have more than one sound are shown in the chart on page 72.

Grapheme		
• Focus on the new grapheme. Put away the other card. • Show the child the picture/ mnemonic side and make a connection between the image and the sound. • Repeat a few times, using the **copy me method**. • Use the digraph/trigraph mantra *'two/three letters, one sound'*. • Show the child the grapheme side of the card as you say the sound. • Draw the letter formation over the grapheme as you say the sound. • Repeat a few times, using the **copy me method**. The child can draw the letter formation over the picture as you say the sound together. • Play the **Grapheme game**. Show alternate sides of the card as the child calls out. Repeat. • Play **Win it!** (one-to-one lessons only; see page 34).	• Give the child their own version of the grapheme card, at an appropriate size, and adapt the card to suit the child's sensory needs. • Either use the sensory grapheme cards or create sensory input by adding textured materials, such as Wikki Stix, over the grapheme so the child can trace over it. • Give the child the appropriate picture card/grapheme to point to in the **Grapheme game** and **Win it!**, if they cannot produce speech sounds.	• Choose graphemes that the child can read securely for **Win it!** (one-to-one lessons only; see page 34). If they don't read a grapheme easily, put it to the side and teach it again in the next session. • Play **Win it!** a few times, putting the new grapheme back several cards each time, to ensure the child has lots of practice. This will help move both pronunciations of the grapheme into their long-term memory. • Write the grapheme on a sticker and stick it on the child's top or sleeve in such a way that they can look down and read both phonemes. • Make sure the child's class teacher and parent/carer are told which graphemes the child is learning with you, so they can practise them with the child at other times.

Blending and reading words

Oral blending games

- Oral blending is an important skill needed for reading, but it is not a prerequisite for learning to blend with graphemes or for learning to read graphemes.
- Children who are not yet able to blend aloud can show their understanding by pointing to the pictures associated with the word.
- You can use the oral blending games with the words on the Phase 2 grapheme chart (pages 62 to 64) as another way of practising this skill with children who cannot blend aloud – yet.
- These activities may need to be repeated several times, to help children hear and say the phonemes and blend the words.

What to do	Appropriate adjustments	Notes
Can you touch your ... ?		
• Tell the children that you are going to play a game where they touch different parts of their body. • Model what will happen. For example, **say**: *Can you touch your h-e-d?* [Touch your head.] • For each word: • Use the **copy me method**. • **Say:** *Can you touch your [name body part]?* Then sound-talk the word twice. • Give feedback. Praise and ask the children to join in with you as you repeat	• For children with limited mobility, adjust the actions, as necessary, to correspond with the types of movement they are able to make. • If a child cannot produce accurate speech or voice sounds, accept the sounds they can make.	• Quickly clear up any misconceptions. (If they touch the wrong part of the body, for example.) • Aim for a lively pace, with lots of expression and warmth to keep the children's interest.
What is making the sound?		
• Tell the children that you are going to play a game about the sounds different animals and things make. • Model what will happen. For example, **say:** *A c-a-t says miaow. [Repeat, then sound-talk and blend.] A c-a-t cat says miaow.* • For each word: • Say the sentence. Sound-talk the blending word. • Repeat. • Say the sentence. Sound-talk the word and blend it. • Ask the children to join in.	• Choose animals and vehicles that are likely to be familiar to the children. If they are unsure what the appropriate noise is, demonstrate it for them. • If a child cannot produce accurate speech or voice sounds, accept the sounds they can make.	• As the children sound-talk the word, nod your head to prompt them with the number of sounds. • Over time, you can give the children less support – by using the **copy me method** but sound-talking the word once only.
Blend from the box		
• Explain to the children that you have some objects in your box and you want them to help you work out what they are. • For each object: • Use the **copy me method**. • Sound-talk the word twice. • Ask the children to sound-talk the word and then blend to say the word. Model sound-talking and blending the word. • Show the children the object and check they know what it is.	• Use objects that give a sensory input where possible. Allow children to feel or hold the object if appropriate. • Start with a small number of objects, which you can increase if appropriate. • If a child cannot produce accurate speech or voice sounds, accept the sounds they can make.	• You will need items or pictures to use in this oral blending game. Suitable words and objects to use can be found in the Phase 2 grapheme chart (see page 62).

Can you do the actions?

• Tell the children that you are going to play an action game.
• Model what will happen. For example, **say:** *Can you c-l-a-p?* [Clap your hands.]
• For each word:
  • **Say:** *Can you [sound-talk the word]?*
  • Give feedback.
  • Repeat.
  • Sound-talk the word. Blend it. Then all do the action together.
	• For children with limited mobility, adjust the actions, as necessary, to correspond with the types of movement they are able to make.
	• If a child cannot produce accurate speech or voice sounds, accept the sounds they can make.
		• As the children sound-talk the word, nod your head to prompt them with the number of sounds.
		• Over time, you can give the children less support – by using the **copy me method** but sound-talking the word once only.

What's that noise?

• Tell the children that you are going to play a game about the sounds made by different things, such as animals or vehicles.
• Model what will happen. For example, **say:** *What sound does a d-o-g make? A d-o-g dog says woof/bark. Let's all bark like a d-o-g!*
• For each word:
  • **Say:** *What sound/noise does a/an [sound-talk the word] make?* Pause and listen to the children.
  • Repeat.
  • Sound-talk the word and make the noise. Ask the children to join in!
	• Choose animals and vehicles that are likely to be familiar to the children. If they are unsure what the appropriate noise is, demonstrate it for them.
	• If a child cannot produce accurate speech or voice sounds, accept the sounds they can make.
		• As the children sound-talk the word, nod your head to prompt them with the number of sounds.
		• Over time, you can give the children less support – by using the **copy me method** but sound-talking the word once only.

Point to the picture/Point to the ...

• Tell the children that you are going to sound-talk the word for each picture and you want them to listen carefully and then point to the correct picture. • Put out four pictures so the children can easily point to them. • Sound-talk the word twice. • Ask the children to sound-talk the word and either blend aloud or in their head, and then point to the picture. • Model sound-talking and blending the word as you give feedback to the children.	• Use images from Little Wandle SEND image banks/eye gaze software/ PECS if appropriate. • If a child cannot produce accurate speech or voice sounds, accept the sounds they can make.	• Use the following **Phase 2 picture cards**: net, duck, cat, sock, kite, bear, box, queen, shell, goat, ring, mouse, snake, or other pictures of single-syllable words (e.g. egg, dog, pen, peg). • You can also use this activity with items in the classroom, for example: *Point to the d-oo-r.*

Blending and reading words – super-supported method

You will need:
- grapheme cards to make the words the child will read.

What to do	Appropriate adjustments	Notes
• Use the grapheme cards and check which GPCs the child can read fluently. Use these GPCs to make up the words for this session. **Model reading the word** • Put out the grapheme cards. • Say the sounds. Pause as if you're thinking. Blend the word slowly, stretching the sounds out to help (e.g. mmmannn). • Say the sounds. Blend the word a bit faster. Then say the word. • Say the sounds. Blend the word at normal speed. Look like you're having a 'lightbulb' moment. Say the word. • Point to each grapheme as you say its phoneme. • Sweep and blend the word. **Together** • Ask the child to join in and point to each grapheme, then say its phoneme, sweep and blend the word. **Child** • Ask the child to have a go at reading. • Ask them to say each phoneme as you point to each grapheme. • Ask them to blend as you sweep beneath the word. • Repeat as needed to ensure over-learning through repetition. **Assess** • If the child is successful, read other words with this method and then try the supported method (see page 43). • If the child is not successful, ask them to read the word with you. Then repeat. • Continuously monitor the child's knowledge and skill levels, and adjust teaching strategies accordingly as the child gradually becomes more successful.	• Think aloud: Model your thinking and support the child in thinking aloud. Foster discussion. • Use objects that give a sensory input. Provide visual aids where possible: when blending c-a-t, have a toy cat. This aids learning and recall. • Use mirrors to help the child see how they make the sound. • Use balloons and other objects that give feedback to help the child feel the sound. • Encourage the child to touch the graphemes as they say them. • Use images from Little Wandle SEND image banks/eye gaze software/PECS if appropriate. **Non-verbal children** • Use the Little Wandle SEND image banks to find images that match the words you are blending. Ask the child to blend and then point to the image that matches the word.	• Choose the method with which the child will be successful – move to a less-supported method during the session if appropriate. • Aim for independent blending with word cards. Gradually increase independent problem-solving as the child becomes more proficient. • Tailor lessons according to the child's existing knowledge and skill. • Make words with GPCs that the child can read with ease. Do not make words with any GPCs that are not secure. • Always show the grapheme side of the cards to make the words. • Make sure the graphemes and words are directly in front of the child. • The child may well find it hard to blend the word successfully, even if they can read the sounds with ease. • They will need daily practice and support to learn to blend – do not give up.

Blending and reading words – supported method

You will need:
- grapheme cards to make the words the child will read.

What to do	Appropriate adjustments	Notes

• Use the grapheme cards and check which GPCs the child can read fluently. Use these GPCs to make up the words for this session.
 	
For each word:
• Put out the cards to make the word.
• Model reading.
  • Read and point to each grapheme.
  • Sweep and blend.
 	
Child
• Ask the child to have a go at reading.
• Ask them to say each phoneme as you point to each grapheme.
• Ask them to blend as you sweep beneath the word.
• Repeat as needed to ensure over-learning through repetition.
 	
Together
• Ask the child to join in and point to each grapheme, then say its phoneme, sweep and blend the word.
 	
Assess
• If the child is successful, read another word with the supported method and then try the whisper method (see page 44).
• If the child is not successful, ask them to read the word with you. Then repeat the whole process for a few other words or go back to the super-supported method (see page 42).
 	
Assess: Mix it up
• Choose two words you have already read.
• For each word:
  • Mix up the cards. Put them into the correct order to make the word.
  • Model reading. Read and point to each grapheme. Sweep and blend.
  • Mix up the cards and give them to the child.
  • Ask the child to put the cards into the correct order to make the word.
  • Ask them to point to each grapheme and say each phoneme.
  • Ask them to sweep beneath the word and blend to read the word.
	• The child may not be able to produce accurate sounds/words themselves; this does not mean that they have not understood the activity.
	• Encourage the child to touch the graphemes as they say them.
	• Metacognition can help children learn. Remind the child how they blend to read words. Ask them to think about how they sound out each sound and then blend the sounds together to say the word.
	
	Pace
	• Include pause points and time to consolidate and check understanding.
	• This activity may need to be repeated several times, to help the child hear the phonemes in the word.
	
	Non-verbal children
	• Use the Little Wandle SEND image banks to find images that match the words you are blending. Ask the child to blend and then point to the image that matches the word.
		• Make words with GPCs that the child can read with ease. Do not make words with any GPCs that are not secure.
		• Always show the grapheme side of the card to make the words.
		• Make sure the graphemes and words are directly in front of the child.
		• The child may well find it hard to blend the word successfully, even if they can read the sounds with ease. They will need daily practice and support to learn to blend – do not give up.
		• You may want to model fewer words each session as the child becomes more confident and moves to the next stage of blending more quickly.
		• The child can take over the pointing and sweeping when they are reading the word, as soon as they are confident and want to!

Blending and reading words – whisper method

You will need:
- grapheme cards to make the words the child will read
- a sticker on which to write words from the session for the child to read later.

What to do	Appropriate adjustments	Notes

• Use the grapheme cards and check which GPCs the child can read fluently. Use these GPCs to make up the words for this session.
 	
For each word:
• Put out the cards to make the word.
• Model reading.
  • Whisper the phonemes and point to each grapheme.
  • Sweep and blend, whispering the word.
 	
Child
• Ask the child to have a go at reading.
• Ask them to say each phoneme as you point to each grapheme.
• Ask them to blend as you sweep beneath the word.
 	
Together
• Ask the child to say each phoneme as you point to each grapheme. Whisper the phoneme to support them as necessary.
• Ask them to blend as you sweep beneath the word. Whisper blend to support them as necessary.
 	
Assess
• If the child is successful, read another word with this method, this time without whisper blending. Then try independent reading (see page 45) with word cards.
• If the child is not successful, ask them to read the word with you.
 	
Assess: Mix it up
• Choose two words you have already read.
• For each word:
  • Mix up the cards. Put them into the correct order to make the word.
  • Model reading. Read and point to each grapheme. Sweep and blend.
  • Mix up the cards and give them to the child.
  • Ask the child to put the cards into the correct order to make the word.
  • Ask them to point to each grapheme and say each phoneme.
  • Ask them to sweep beneath the word and blend to read the word.
	• The child may not be able to produce accurate sounds/words themselves; accept the sounds they make.
	• Encourage the child to touch the graphemes as they say them.
	• Move to independent blending and reading (page 45) only the child is able to sound out and blend the words without whisper blending.
	• Metacognition can help children learn. Remind the child how they blend to read words. Ask them to think about how they sound out each sound and then blend the sounds together to say the word.
	
	Pace
	• Include pause points and time to consolidate and check understanding.
	• This activity may need to be repeated several times, to help the child hear the phonemes in the word. Little and often is usually best!
	
	Non-verbal children
	• Use the Little Wandle SEND image banks to find images that match the words you are blending. Ask the child to blend and then point to the image that matches the word.
		• Make words with GPCs that the child can read with ease. Do not make words with any GPCs that are not secure.
		• Always show the grapheme side of the card to make the words.
		• Make sure the graphemes and words are directly in front of the child.
		• You may want to model fewer words each session as the child becomes more confident and moves to the next stage of blending more quickly.
		• The child can take over the pointing and sweeping when they are reading the word as soon as they are confident and want to!
		• This is the bridge to independent reading. Make sure the child has a go at reading a word without any support – with the grapheme cards – in every session.
		• Write two words from the session on a sticker and stick it on the child's top or sleeve in such a way that they can look down and read it.
		• Make sure the parents/carers are told which GPCs the child is making words with, so they can practise them with the child at other times.

Blending and reading words – independent reading

You will need:
- Phase 2, 3, 4 or 5 word cards
- Phase 2, 3 or 5 grapheme cards for a quick review
- four to six words the child can read with confidence as the review pack for **Win it!**
- a sticker on which to write a word for the child after the session.

What to do	Appropriate adjustments	Notes

• Start the session with a quick review of Phase 2, 3 or 5 GPCs using the grapheme cards.
 • For each word:
   • Put the word card (sound button side up) in front of the child.
   • If applicable, ask if they can see any digraphs in the word.
 	
 Child
 • Ask the child to sound-talk each grapheme and then blend to read the word aloud.
 • Ask them to point to each grapheme and then sweep beneath as they blend. Do not help them.
 	
 Together
 • Ask the child to join in and point to each grapheme, then say its phoneme together, sweep and blend the word. This aids fluency and helps the child hear the word pronounced correctly.
 	
 Assess
 • If the child is successful, read another word with this method, using the word cards.
 • If the child is confident, challenge them to read without overt blending. Model blending in your head to read the word aloud, then ask them to have a go themselves.
 • If the child is not successful, ask them to read the word with you and then go back to the whisper method (see page 44) to support them.
	• Use enlarged word cards if needed.
	 • Where possible, use images from the Little Wandle SEND image banks or appropriate images from eye gaze software/PECS to help the child link the word to its meaning.
	 • The child may not be able to produce accurate sounds/ words themselves; accept the sounds they make.
	 • Encourage the child to touch the graphemes as they say them.
	 • Return to blending using the whisper method (page 44) if the child is struggling to sound out and blend the words independently.
	 • Metacognition can help children learn. Remind the child how they blend to read words. Ask them to think about how they sound out each sound and then blend the sounds together to say the word.
		• Only use words with GPCs that the child can read with ease. Do not make words with any GPCs that are not secure.
		
		 Phase 2
		 • Start with words that do not have digraphs.
		 • When the child is confident reading these words, start to use words with the Phase 2 digraphs 'ck', 'll', 'ff', 'ss', 'zz', 'qu', 'th', 'ch', 'sh', 'ng' and 'nk'.
		
		 Phases 3 to 5
		 • Start with words that only have graphemes from the previous phase (i.e. Phase 2 digraphs if in Phase 3, etc.)
		 • When the child is confident reading these words, progress to words including graphemes from the child's current phase.
		 • If the child is confident, challenge them to read without overt blending – blending in their head to read the word aloud.
		 • Write one word from the session on a sticker and stick it on the child's top or sleeve in such a way that they can look down and read it.
		 • Make sure the parents/carers are told which GPCs the child is making words with, so they can practise them with the child at other times.

Win it! (one-to-one lessons only) • Use the side of the word card without sound buttons for this activity. • Add one of the new word cards to the review pack. Make sure it is close to the top of the pack. • Each time the child reads the new word correctly, the game stops and they 'win' the card. • Ask the child to give you the card back to see if they can win it again. • Shuffle and repeat, incrementally moving the new card back. • You can add another word to the pack if there is time.	• Give the child the appropriate picture card/grapheme to point to in **Win it!**, if they cannot produce speech sounds.	• Have a pack of four to six words the child can read with confidence as the review pack for **Win it!**

All Phases: Reading tricky words

You will need:
- a tricky word to learn and four to six tricky words that the child already knows for **Win it!**
- a sticker on which to write one tricky word for the child after the session.

What to do	Appropriate adjustments	Notes
• Show the tricky word on a card. Read the decodable parts of the word. Point to the 'tricky bit' and tell the child the sound that this grapheme makes. • Model reading the word. • Ask the child to read the word a few times independently	• Use enlarged word cards if needed. • The child may not be able to produce accurate sounds/ words themselves; accept the sounds they make. • Ensure that the child knows the meaning of each tricky word, and model how to use the word in a sentence. • Encourage the child to point to each grapheme and then sweep beneath as they blend. • Adjust the number of words as necessary to support the child – you could start with just one or two words and increase the number if the child reads these successfully. • This activity may need to be repeated many times to embed the reading of tricky words – little and often is usually best!	• Write one word from the session on a sticker and stick it on the child's top or sleeve in such a way that they can look down and read it. • Make sure the class teacher and parent/carer are told which words the child is reading in these sessions, so they can practise them with the child at other times
Win it! (One-to-one lessons only) • Add the new tricky word card to the review pack. Make sure it is close to the top of the pack. • Each time the child reads the new word correctly, they 'win' the card. Stop the game, and the child returns the card to you. Shuffle the cards and move the new tricky word card back a bit in the pack. • Shuffle and repeat, incrementally moving the new card back. • You can add another word to the pack if there is time.	• Give the child the appropriate picture card/ grapheme to point to in **Win it!**, if they cannot produce speech sounds.	• Have a pack of four to six tricky words the children can read with confidence as the review pack for **Win it!**

All phases: Reading words with speedy digraph/trigraph recognition

You will need:
- Phase 2, 3 and 5 grapheme cards for a quick review
- Phase 2, 3, 4 and 5 word cards
- word cards with graphemes the child can read fluently, for **Win it!**
- a sticker on which to write the word for the child to read after the session.

What to do	Appropriate adjustments	Notes
• Start the session with a quick review of GPCs using the Phase 2 and 3 or Phase 5 grapheme cards. • For each word: • Put the word card (show side without sound buttons) in front of the children. • Ask if they can see any digraphs in the word. If they cannot, show them the appropriate grapheme card, remind them what it says, and point to the matching grapheme in the word. **Children** • Ask the children to sound-talk each grapheme and then blend to read the word aloud. • Ask them to point to each grapheme and then sweep beneath as they blend. Do not help them. **Together** • Ask the children to join in as they point to each grapheme and say its phoneme, sweep and blend the word. **Assess** • If the child is successful, read another word with this method. • If they continue to find it difficult to identify the digraphs/trigraphs, model the process using the whisper method (see page 44).	• Use enlarged word cards if needed. • The child may not be able to produce accurate sounds/words themselves; accept the sounds they make. • Use words that are meaningful to the child wherever possible. Ensure that the child knows the meaning of each word, and model how to use the word in a sentence if it is unfamiliar. • Where possible use images from Little Wandle SEND image banks or appropriate images from eye gaze software/PECS to help children link the word to its meaning. • Return to blending with the whisper method (see page 44) if the child is struggling to sound out and blend the words independently. • Metacognition can help children learn. Remind the child how they blend to read words. Ask them to think about how they sound out each sound and then blend the sounds together to read the word.	• Only use words with Phase 2, 3 or 5 digraphs/trigraphs that the children can read with ease. • Use words with one digraph only to start with (e.g. seed, green). Build up to words with more than one digraph (e.g. sheep) once these words are secure. • Choose four to six words to read in the session. • Put aside any GPCs that the children cannot read automatically. • Ensure these GPCs are taught in the next session using 'Teaching a Phase 2, 3 or 5 digraph' and/or precision teaching. • Do not stop teaching these GPCs until they are all automatic. • Write one word from the session on a sticker and stick it on the children's top or sleeve in such a way that they can look down and read it. • Make sure the class teacher and parent/carer are told which words the children is reading in these sessions, so they can practise them
Win it! (One-to-one lessons only) • Use the side of the word card without sound buttons for this activity. • Add one of the new word cards to the review pack. Make sure it is close to the top of the pack. • Each time the child reads the new word, stop the game, shuffle the cards and move the card back a bit in the pack. • Shuffle and repeat, incrementally moving the new card back. • Each time the child reads the new word correctly, they 'win' the card. • You can add another word to the pack if there is time.	• Give the child the appropriate picture card/grapheme to point to in **Win it!** if they cannot produce speech sounds.	• Have a pack of four to six words the children can read with confidence as the review pack for **Win it!**

Phase 4: Reading words with adjacent consonants

You will need:
- Phase 2 and 3 grapheme cards to make the words the child will read
- Phase 4 word cards, if the child progresses to independent reading
- a sticker on which to write one word for the child after the session.

What to do	Appropriate adjustments	Notes
• Use the Phase 2 and 3 grapheme cards to check which GPCs the child can read fluently. Use these GPCs to make up the words for this session. • For each word: 　• Put out the cards to make the word. 　• Model reading. Whisper and point to each grapheme. Sweep and blend. **Child** • Ask the child to have a go at reading. • Ask them to say each phoneme as you point to each grapheme. • Ask them to blend as you sweep beneath the word. **Together** • Ask the child to join in as you point to each grapheme and whisper its phoneme, then sweep and blend the word. **Assess** • If the child is successful, read another word, this time without whisper blending, and then try independent reading (see page 45) with word cards. • If the child is not successful, ask them to read the word with you. Then repeat the whole process for a few other words. **Assess: Mix it up** • Choose two words you have already read. • For each word: 　• Mix up the grapheme cards. Put them into the correct order to make the word. 　• Model reading. Read and point to each grapheme. Sweep and blend. 　• Mix up the cards and give them to the child. 　• Ask the child to put the cards into the correct order to make the word. 　• Ask them to point to each grapheme and say each phoneme. 　• Ask them to sweep beneath the word and blend to read the word.	• Use enlarged grapheme and word cards if needed. • The child may not be able to produce accurate sounds/words themselves; accept the sounds they make. • Use words that are meaningful to the child wherever possible. Ensure that the child knows the meaning of each word, and model how to use the word in a sentence if it is unfamiliar. • Where possible use images from Little Wandle SEND image banks or appropriate images from eye gaze software/PECS to help the child link the word to its meaning. • Return to supported blending (see page 43) if the child is struggling to sound out and blend the words independently. • Metacognition can help children learn. Remind the child how they blend to read words. Ask them to think about how they sound out each sound and then blend the sounds together to read the word.	• You can some a list of the word types covered in Phase 4 and some example words on page 20. • Start by making words with adjacent consonants and short vowel sounds. • Words with two adjacent consonants at the end (e.g. went, help) are easier to start with. • Move to two adjacent consonants at the beginning of words (e.g. drum, smell), before reading words with three adjacent consonants (e.g. strap, strong). • If needed, repeat the process with adjacent consonants and long vowel sounds. • Write one word from the session on a sticker and stick it on the child's top or sleeve in such a way that they can look down and read it later. • Make sure the class teacher and parent/carer are told which words the child is reading in these sessions, so they can practise them with the child at other times.

Phases 3, 4 and 5: Reading longer words

You will need:
- Phase 3 or 4 word cards with words of more than one syllable
- other Phase 3 or 4 words that the child can read confidently, for the **Win it!** review pack
- a sticker on which to write one word for the child after the session.

What to do	Appropriate adjustments	Notes
• Select a word to start with. **Model chunking the first word (e.g. ladder)** • Cover the second part of the word (so the card shows 'ladd'). • Sound-talk the first part of the word using the point and sweep actions: l-a-dd lad • Reveal the second part of the word (-er) and repeat the step above. • Blend as you sweep under the whole word: ladder. **Child** • Put the card in front of the child and cover the second part of the word. • Ask the child to sound-talk each grapheme and then blend the first part of the word aloud. • Reveal the second part of the word and repeat the step above. • Ask the child to point to each grapheme and then sweep beneath as they blend the whole word. If the child is not successful, do it together then ask them to try again alone. **Together** • Ask the child to join in and point to each grapheme, then say its phoneme together, sweep and blend the word. This aids fluency and helps the child hear the word pronounced correctly. **For each subsequent word** • Put the word card in front of the child. • Ask the child to identify the trigraphs/digraphs. • Cover the second part of the word. • Ask the child to sound-talk each grapheme and then blend the first part of the word aloud. • Reveal the second part of the word and repeat the step above. • Ask the child to point to each grapheme and then sweep beneath as they blend the whole word. If the child is not successful, do it together then ask them to try again alone. • If the child is unable to read the word independently, repeat the 'Together' step above.	• Use enlarged grapheme and word cards if needed. • The child may not be able to produce accurate sounds/words themselves; accept the sounds they make. • Use words that are meaningful to the child wherever possible. Ensure that the child knows the meaning of each word, and model how to use the word in a sentence if it is unfamiliar. • Where possible use images from Little Wandle SEND image banks or appropriate images from eye gaze software/PECS to help the child link the word to its meaning. • Adjust the number of words as necessary to support the child – you could start with just one or two words and increase the number if the child reads these successfully. • Return to blending using the whisper method (see page 44) if the child is struggling to sound out and blend the words independently. • Metacognition can help children learn. Remind the child how they blend to read words. Ask them to think about how they sound out each sound and then blend the sounds together to read the word.	• Choose four or five words to read in a session. • Model the procedure for the first word, to ensure the child knows what to do. • Always cover up the syllables for the child as they won't be able to work these out for themselves. • Write one word from the session on a sticker and stick it on the child's top or sleeve in such a way that they can look down and read it later. • Make sure the class teacher and parent/carer are told which words the child is reading in these sessions, so they can practise them with the child at other times.
Win it! (one-to-one lessons only) • See page 45.		

Phase 5: Reading words with graphemes that have more than one sound, e.g. 'ow' /ow/ /oa/

You will need:

- Phase 3 grapheme card (picture side)
- SEND Phase 5 grapheme card for the same grapheme
- Phase 3, 4 and 5 word cards for the grapheme you are teaching
- images to support the word cards where possible
- stickers to write the words on – one for each sound the grapheme makes – for the child after the session.

What to do	Appropriate adjustments	Notes
Revise the new phoneme • Remind the child that the grapheme (e.g. 'ow') makes more than one sound (e.g. /ow/ and /oa/). • Display the picture side of the Phase 3 grapheme card and the picture side of the SEND Phase 5 grapheme card that matches the new sound that you are teaching for the same grapheme, e.g. for 'ow', display /ow/ 'wow owl' and /oa/ 'rainbow'. • Point to each card. Say the catchphrase, e.g. /ow/ 'wow owl' and the word 'rainbow', to help the child really hear the two different phonemes. • Tell the child to say the correct sound as you point to the images.	• Use enlarged grapheme cards if needed. • Use a mirror to help the child see how they make the sound. • Use balloons and other objects that give feedback, to help the child feel the sound. • If the child cannot produce accurate speech sounds, accept the sounds they can make.	• This activity is for children who can identify the graphemes but find attributing the correct phoneme difficult. • If a child cannot identify the digraphs with ease, use the Prompt card **Reading words with speedy digraph/trigraph recognition** (page 47). • See the list of Phase 5 graphemes with more than one sound on page 72.
Sort the words by phoneme • Show the picture side of the Phase 3 and Phase 5 grapheme cards. • Tell the child they will now read words and work out which picture they should go under, according to the sound the grapheme makes. For each word: • Put the word card in front of the child. Use the side without sound buttons if you think the child can read the word independently; use the side with sound buttons if the child needs more support. • Ask them to identify the grapheme. • Read each word. Begin by reading a word and asking the child to sort it under the correct picture. • When the child is confident, move to them reading the word independently before sorting it. • If the child reads the word with the incorrect pronunciation for the grapheme, model the correct pronunciation and return the word to the pack for the child to try later.	• Use enlarged word cards if needed. • The child may not be able to produce accurate sounds/words themselves; accept the sounds they make. • Ensure that the child knows the meaning of each word, and model how to use the word in a sentence if it is unfamiliar. • Use objects that give a sensory input. Provide visual aids where possible: when blending 'snake', have a toy snake. This aids learning and recall. • Metacognition can help children learn. Remind the child how they blend to read words. Ask them to think about how they sound out each sound and then blend the sounds together to read the word.	• Use six to eight words for this activity. Use words without sound buttons if the child is confident enough to read the words independently; use words with sound buttons if they need more support. • Some words have more than one pronunciation, e.g. 'read', 'wind'. Discuss these with the child and use them in contextualising sentences. • Encourage the child to think about words they know, and what would make sense, when they are trying to work out which of two phonemes to use for a grapheme. For example, for 'rainbow', if they try both r-ai-n-b-ow and r-ai-n-b-oa, and think about which sounds like a real word, they may realise it must be 'ow' /oa/. Using pictures to support the words can help with this, too. • Make a sticker with two words from the session, one for each sound the grapheme makes, and stick it on the child's top or sleeve so they can look down and read it later. • Make sure the class teacher and parent/carer are told which words the child is reading in these sessions, so that they can practise them with the child at other times.

Phase 5: Reading words containing a split vowel digraph

You will need:

- Phase 5 split vowel digraph words.

What to do	Appropriate adjustments	Notes

• Model how to read the first word (e.g. home).
 • Show the word card (sound buttons showing).
 • Read each sound as you point. Point to the arch as you read the split vowel digraph.
 • Sweep beneath as you blend the whole word.
 • Tell the child that the arch shows that the two letters are making one sound, even though they are not next to each other.
 	
 Child
 • Ask the child to sound-talk each grapheme and then blend to read the word aloud.
 • Ask them to point to each grapheme and then sweep beneath as they blend. Do not help them.
 • For each subsequent word:
  • Put the word card in front of the child.
  • Ask if they can see any digraphs/split vowel digraphs in the word.
  • Ask them to point to each grapheme and then sweep beneath as they blend. If the child is not successful, do it together then ask them to try again alone.
 	
 Together
 • Ask the child to join in to read the word by blending 'in their head'. Sweep beneath the word as you read.
 • Aim to read the words without overt blending as described below.
 • For each word:
  • Put the word card in front of the child.
  • Ask them to point to any digraphs/ split vowel digraphs in the word and say what they are.
  • Tell the child to read the words on the cards without sounding out.
  • Ask them to sweep beneath the word as they read.
  • Repeat.
	• Use enlarged word cards if needed.
	 • The child may not be able to produce accurate sounds/words themselves; accept the sounds they make.
	 • Use words that are meaningful to the child wherever possible. Ensure that the child knows the meaning of each word, and model how to use the word in a sentence if it is unfamiliar.
	 • Where possible use images from the image bank or appropriate images from eye gaze software/ PECS to help children link the word to its meaning.
	 • Return to blending using the whisper method (see page 44) if the child is struggling to sound out and blend the words independently.
	 • Metacognition can help children learn. Remind the child how they blend to read words. Ask them to think about how they sound out each sound and then blend the sounds together to read the word.
		• Use the word cards with the sound buttons.
		 • Over time, move to showing the words without the sound buttons, so the child becomes expert at spotting the split vowel digraph.
		 • Ensure lots of repetition so the child becomes confident in reading these types of words.
		 • Aim for the child to read the words without overt blending, so they are growing in fluency and accuracy.

Practise and apply

All phases: Mix it up (spelling with grapheme cards – one-to-one)

You will need:

- grapheme cards for the phase that you are working on.

What to do	Appropriate adjustments	Notes

• Display the grapheme cards you need to spell the word, as well as some extra grapheme cards as distractors.
 	
Oral practice
• Use the **copy me method** to say the word and then segment it.
• Count the sounds in the word.
 	
Spelling with grapheme cards
• Model spelling the word with grapheme cards:
  • Segment the word and choose the correct grapheme for the first sound.
  • Place the card on the table.
  • Continue with all the sounds until you have spelled the word.
  • Read the word.
• Mix up the cards and ask the child to spell the word independently by segmenting and choosing the correct graphemes.
• Ask the child to read the word.
	• Use enlarged grapheme cards if needed.
	• The child may not be able to produce accurate sounds/words themselves; accept the sounds they make.
	• Use words that are meaningful to the child wherever possible. Ensure that the child knows the meaning of each word, and model how to use the word in a sentence if it is unfamiliar.
		• This activity works best in a one-to-one session but you could try it with pairs or a small group if you have enough grapheme cards.
		• Use segmenting fingers to support the child to segment sounds.
		• If there is a digraph/trigraph, use the mantra *'two/three letters, one sound'*.

All phases: Spelling (without grapheme cards)

You will need:

- mini whiteboards and pens.

What to do	Appropriate adjustments	Notes
• Use the **copy me method** to say the word and then segment it. • Count the sounds in the word. • Model spelling the word. • Ask the child to say each sound before you write it down. If there is a digraph/trigraph, use the mantra *'two/three letters, one sound'* to remind the child. Say the letter name after you write it. • Hide the word. • Ask the child to spell the word. Tell them to segment as they write. • Show your spelling and check together. • Repeat if there are other words to spell.	• The child may not be able to produce accurate sounds/words themselves; accept the sounds they make. • Use words that are meaningful to the child wherever possible. Ensure that the child knows the meaning of each word, and model how to use the word in a sentence if it is unfamiliar. • Use segmenting fingers to support the child to segment sounds.	• Use segmenting fingers to support the child to segment sounds. • Minimise your language but remind the child to segment as they write. • Observe and support the child as they write. Ensure they use correct letter formation but do not let this detract from the lesson. (Handwriting must be taught as a separate lesson.) **Spelling tricky words:** Use the same method as for spelling decodable words but point out the 'tricky bit' as you identify the sounds and write them down.

Phases 4 and 5: Change it

You will need:

- grapheme cards for the phase you are working on.

What to do	Appropriate adjustments	Notes

Change it
- For each word:
  - Put out the cards to make the word.
  - Ask the child to sound-talk each grapheme and then blend to read the word aloud.
  - Point to each grapheme and then sweep beneath the word to signal blending. Do not help the child.
  - Look at the child (not at the card).
  - Read the word together.
- **Say:** *Change it.* Take one grapheme away and replace it with the new grapheme to change the word.
- Ask the child to read the new grapheme. Remind them of what the word said before. **Say:** *Now let's read a new word.*
- Repeat the procedure above.
	- Use enlarged grapheme cards if needed.
	- The child may not be able to produce accurate sounds/words themselves; accept the sounds they make.
	- Use words that are meaningful to the child wherever possible. Ensure that the child knows the meaning of each word, and model how to use the word in a sentence if it is unfamiliar.
		- You will need the grapheme cards to make all the words listed in the weekly grid.
		- Follow the order of the words listed in the weekly grid, so that the words change by one grapheme at a time.
		- Use this time to help the child practise blending with less support from you – but if they struggle at all, go back to the teacher-led blending method to ensure they are blending successfully.
		- This activity helps children to see how the graphemes within the word affect how the word sounds. It should help them to identify individual sounds in all parts of the word.
		- This activity will aid reading and spelling skills.

Phases 4 and 5: Match the words to the pictures

You will need:

- the **Match the words to the pictures** resource for the phase that you are working on.

What to do	Appropriate adjustments	Notes

- Display the numbered pictures and then hide them.
- Hold up each word and ask the child to:
  - identify the digraphs/trigraphs
  - read the word (after they have read the word, reveal the pictures again)
  - show which picture matches the word by holding up the appropriate number of fingers.
- Read the word again without any overt blending.
	- Use enlarged grapheme cards if needed.
	- The child may not be able to produce accurate sounds/words themselves; accept the sounds they make.
	- Use words that are meaningful to the child wherever possible. Ensure that the child knows the meaning of each word, and model how to use the word in a sentence if it is unfamiliar.
		- Ensure the child knows what all the pictures represent.

Phases 4 and 5: Read the sentence

You will need:

- a copy of the phrase or sentence for children to read (see weekly grids), written in advance of the lesson on a flipchart or large sheet of paper (or from the website).

What to do	Appropriate adjustments	Notes

- Display the phrase or sentence.
- Ask the child to identify any digraphs they can see. Take feedback.
- Point to the words with digraphs.
- Ask the child to read one or two of the words. Do not read the words to the child.
 	
Tricky words
- Ask the child to identify any tricky words they can see.
- Point to the tricky words and ask the child to read them.
 	
Child reads
- Ask the child to read aloud as you point to the words. Remind them to sound out any words they are not sure of.
 	
Second read
- Ask the child to read again.
 	
Read together
- Read the phrase or sentence together.
- Point to each word. Read at a steady pace.
	- Enlarge the displayed phrase or sentence as appropriate.
	- Ensure that the child knows the meanings of all the words. Explain the meanings and/ or show matching images if necessary to support comprehension.
	- After reading, check that the child has understood the sentence by commenting on it and inviting them to respond/ add their own ideas.
		- When asking the child to read the words:
		  - Sweep underneath the word so that you can then read it together.
		  - As you read together, sweep underneath longer words.
		- Draw the child's attention to the capital letters and full stops in sentences.
		- If you are working with more than one child, pause and ask individual children to read key words (i.e. words including a new grapheme) in the phrase or sentence.

All phases: Precision teaching

- Use this activity to give children repeated practice after initial teaching, which will help them gain fluency and aid automatic recall of GPCs.
- You can also use this precision teaching method with words and tricky words – just set up the grid with the appropriate words that need additional practice.

You will need:

- the grapheme card for the GPC you are teaching
- a copy of the **Precision teaching grids** (see page 61).

In advance of the lesson:

- Write the focus grapheme at least twice in each row, in random places.
- Write three other graphemes that the child knows fluently into the other spaces on the grid.

What to do	Appropriate adjustments	Notes
Focus grapheme • Show the child the grapheme side of the grapheme card. Draw the letter formation over the grapheme as you say the sound. • Repeat a few times, using the **copy me method**. • The child can draw or trace the letter formation over the grapheme as you say the sound together. **Grapheme grid** • Put the filled-in grapheme grid in front of the child. • Model pointing to the focus grapheme on the grid and reading it aloud. • Point to the focus grapheme on the grid and ask the child to read. • Ask the child to find the focus grapheme, point to it and read. • Now ask the child to read all the graphemes in each line as you point. • If the child doesn't recognise a grapheme, tell them the sound, get them to repeat and continue. • Repeat, building on fluency.	**Focus grapheme** • Give the child their own version of the grapheme card, at an appropriate size, and adapt the card to suit the child's sensory needs. • Either use the sensory grapheme cards or create sensory input by adding textured materials, such as Wikki Stix, over the grapheme so the child can trace over it. **Grapheme grid** • Use enlarged grapheme cards and an enlarged grid if needed. • You could use eye gaze software to display the grapheme grid. • The child may not be able to produce accurate sounds/words themselves; accept the sounds they make.	• You can also use the Phase 2 and 3 Grapheme mat to point to graphemes that the child needs to practise to gain fluency. • Choose up to four graphemes to practise, and point to them in random order on the mat. • This method can be used with words as well as GPCs.

Lesson templates

Phase 2 blending practice template

You will need:
- Phase 2 grapheme cards to make the words
- Phase 2 blending words for independent reading
- props for the oral blending game **Blend from the box**.

Revisit and review	Practise and apply	Teach and practise

Oral blending games
- Start the session with a lively oral blending game to tune the children into listening, for example **Blend from the box**.
- See the Prompt cards on pages 40 to 41 or the 'How to' videos for oral blending games for instructions.
 	
Review GPCs
Ask the children to read speedy sounds.
- Use all the cards – grapheme side only. (Only show the mnemonic side if the children are unsure.)
- Do not continue if the children cannot read these GPCs.
- If the GPCs are not secure, teach them as a matter of urgency.
- Do not attempt to teach blending with GPCs that the children cannot read.
	Oral blending
	- Use the **copy me method** to blend three words with the new sound.
	- Ensure the children understand the meaning of each new word.
	
	Teacher-led blending
	Use the appropriate level of support, giving less support as the children become more confident with blending. See the blending Prompt cards on pages 42 to 45 for guidance.
	
	- Use the grapheme cards to make the words. For each word:
	  - Model: Read and point to each grapheme. Sweep and blend.
	  - Use the **copy me method** to repeat the process with the children.
	  - Check and read each word together, giving less support. Watch and assess the children.
		Spelling
		Spell two words and choose either **Mix it up** (for one-to-one sessions) or **Spelling** (for one-to-one sessions or groups) – whichever is appropriate for the children.
		
		Mix it up (spelling with grapheme cards – one-to-one)
		Display the grapheme cards you need to spell the word, as well as some extra grapheme cards as distractors (if appropriate for the child).
		
		Use the **copy me method** to say the word and then segment it.
		- Count the sounds in the word.
		- Model spelling the word:
		  - Segment the word and choose the correct grapheme for the first sound.
		  - Place the card on the table.
		  - Continue with all the sounds until you have spelled the word.
		  - Blend and read the word.
		- Mix up the cards and ask the child to spell the word by segmenting and choosing the correct graphemes.
		- Ask the child to blend and read the word.
		- Repeat for the other word.
		
		Spelling (without grapheme cards)
		- Use the **copy me method** to:
		  - Say the word.
		  - Segment it.
		  - Segment and count the sounds on your fingers.
		- Model spelling the word.
		  - Say the word and how many sounds you need to spell it.
		  - Write each grapheme.
		  - Hide the word.
		- Ask the children to spell the word.
		- Check the word together.
		- Ask the children to check and correct their spelling.
		- Repeat for the other word.

Phase 3 blending practice template

You will need:
- Phase 2 and 3 grapheme cards to make the words
- Phase 3 blending words for independent reading
- word cards, as listed in the lesson
- a flip chart to model spelling
- writing materials for the children.

Revisit and review	Practise and apply	Teach and practise

Quick review
• Ask the children to read speedy sounds.
• Use all the cards – grapheme side only. (Only show the mnemonic side if the children are unsure.)
• Do not continue if the children cannot read these GPCs.
• If the GPCs are not secure, teach them as a matter of urgency.
• Do not attempt to teach blending with GPCs that the children cannot read.
 	
Review focus grapheme
• Use the **copy me method** to practise pronunciation of the focus grapheme. Repeat.
• Show the mnemonic side of the grapheme card to make a connection between the image and the sound, or review the catchphrase.
• Repeat several times.
• Use the **copy me method**. Show the grapheme. Trace over it as you say its sound. Repeat.
• Use the mantra 'two letters, one sound'. Then say the sound.
	Oral blending
	• Use the **copy me method** to blend three words with the new sound.
	• Ensure the children understand the meaning of each new word.
	
	Teacher-led blending
	Use the appropriate level of support, giving less support as the children become more confident with blending. See the blending Prompt cards on pages 42 to 45 for guidance.
	
	• Use the grapheme cards to make the words. For each word:
	  • Model: Read and point to each grapheme. Sweep and blend.
	  • Use the **copy me method** to repeat the process with the children.
	  • Check and read each word together, giving less support. Watch and assess the children.
	
	Once the children can blend without support use independent reading words.
	
	Independent reading
	• Use word cards.
	• Show the word.
	• Point to each grapheme and then sweep to indicate blending.
	• Do not help the children. Look at the children and not the card.
	• Model reading the word.
	• Use pictures, props and simple definitions to ensure the children understand the meaning of each new word.
		Spelling
		Spell two words and choose either **Mix it up** (for one-to-one sessions) or **Spelling** (for one-to-one sessions or groups) – whichever is appropriate for the children.
		
		Mix it up (spelling with grapheme cards – one-to-one)
		Display the grapheme cards you need to spell the word, as well as some extra grapheme cards as distractors (if appropriate for the child).
		
		Use the **copy me method** to say the word and then segment it.
		• Count the sounds in the word.
		• Model spelling the word:
		  • Segment the word and choose the correct grapheme for the first sound.
		  • Place the card on the table.
		  • Continue with all the sounds until you have spelled the word.
		  • Blend and read the word.
		• Mix up the cards and ask the child to spell the word by segmenting and choosing the correct graphemes.
		• Ask the child to blend and read the word.
		• Repeat for the other word.
		
		Spelling (without grapheme cards)
		• Use the **copy me method** to:
		  • Say the word.
		  • Segment it.
		  • Segment and count the sounds on your fingers.
		• Model spelling the word.
		  • Say the word and how many sounds you need to spell it.
		  • Write each grapheme.
		  • Hide the word.
		• Ask the children to spell the word.
		• Check the word together.
		• Ask the children to check and correct their spelling.
		• Repeat for the other word.

Phase 4 lesson template

You will need:
- Phase 4 word cards
- tricky word cards
- grapheme cards for spelling
- images for **Match the words to the pictures**.

Revisit and review	Practise and apply	Teach and practise

Oral blending games
• Start the session with a lively oral blending game to tune the children into listening.
• See the Prompt cards on pages 40 to 41 or the 'How to' videos for oral blending games for guidance.
	Oral blending
	• Use the **copy me method** to blend three words with adjacent consonants.
	• Ensure the children understand the meaning of each new word.
	
	Teacher-led blending
	Use the appropriate level of support, giving less support as the children become more confident with blending. See the blending Prompt cards on pages 42 to 45 for guidance.
	
	• Use the grapheme cards to make the words. For each word:
	  • Model: Read and point to each grapheme. Sweep and blend.
	  • Use the **copy me method** to repeat the process with the children.
	  • Check and read each word together, giving less support. Watch and assess the children.
	
	Once the children can blend without support, use independent reading words.
	
	Independent reading
	• Use word cards.
	• Show the word.
	• Point to each grapheme and then sweep to indicate blending.
	• Do not help the children. Look at the children and not the card.
	• Model reading the word.
	• Use pictures, props and simple definitions to ensure the children understand the meaning of each new word.
		Spelling
		Spell two words and choose either **Mix it up** (for one-to-one sessions) or **Spelling** (for one-to-one sessions or groups) – whichever is appropriate for the children. See the Prompt cards on page 52 for guidance.
		
		Change it
		• Make each word using the grapheme cards.
		• Point to each grapheme and then sweep to indicate blending. Do not help the children.
		• Look at the children (not the cards) and assess.
		• Model reading the word.
		• Change one grapheme in the word (see the weekly grid for the order of the changes) and repeat.
		
		Match the words to the pictures
		• Display the numbered pictures.
		• For each word:
		  • Ask the children to identify the digraphs. Take feedback.
		  • Ask the children to read the word.
		  • Ask them to tell you which picture matches the word by holding up the appropriate number of fingers.

Phase 5 lesson template

You will need:
- Phase 2 and 3 grapheme cards and SEND Phase 5 grapheme cards
- Phase 5 word cards
- tricky word cards
- images for **Match the words to the pictures**.

Revisit and review	Practise and apply	Teach and practise

Quick review
• Ask the children to read speedy sounds.
• Use all the cards – grapheme side only. (Only show the mnemonic side if the children are unsure.)
• Do not continue if the children cannot read these GPCs.
• If the GPCs are not secure, teach them as a matter of urgency.
• Do not attempt to teach blending or word reading with GPCs that the children cannot read.
 	
Review focus graphemes
• Use the **copy me method** to practise pronunciation of the focus grapheme. Repeat.
• Show the picture side of the grapheme card to make a connection between the image and the sound.
• Repeat several times.
• Use the **copy me method**. Show the grapheme.
• Use the mantra *'two letters, one sound'*. Then say the sound.
	Oral blending
	• Use the **copy me method** to blend three words with adjacent consonants.
	• Ensure the children understand the meaning of each new word.
	
	Teacher-led blending
	Use the appropriate level of support, giving less support as the children become more confident with blending. See the blending Prompt cards on pages 42 to 45 for guidance.
	
	• Use the grapheme cards to make the words. For each word:
	  • Model: Read and point to each grapheme. Sweep and blend.
	  • Use the **copy me method** to repeat the process with the children.
	  • Check and read each word together, giving less support. Watch and assess the children.
	
	Once the children can blend without support, use independent reading words.
		Spelling
		Spell two words and choose either **Mix it up** (for one-to-one sessions) or **Spelling** (for one-to-one sessions or groups) – whichever is appropriate for the children.
		
		Mix it up (spelling with grapheme cards)
		Display the grapheme cards you need to spell the word, as well as some extra grapheme cards as distractors (if appropriate for the child).
		
		• Use the **copy me method** to say the word and then segment it.
		• Count the sounds in the word.
		• Model spelling the word:
		  • Segment the word and choose the correct grapheme for the first sound.
		  • Place the card on the table.
		  • Continue with all the sounds until you have spelled the word.
		  • Blend and read the word.
		• Mix up the cards and ask the child to spell the word by segmenting and choosing the correct graphemes.
		• Ask the child to blend and read the word.
		• Repeat for the other word.
		
		Spelling (without grapheme cards)
		• Use the **copy me method** to:
		  • Say the word.
		  • Segment it.
		  • Segment and count the sounds.
		• Model spelling the word.
		  • Say the word and how many sounds you need to spell it.
		  • Write each grapheme.
		  • Hide the word.
		• Ask the children to spell the word.
		• Check the word together.
		• Ask the children to check and correct their spelling.
		• Repeat for the other word.
		
		Match the words to the pictures
		• Display the numbered pictures.
		• For each word:
		  • Ask the children to identify the digraphs. Take feedback.
		  • Ask the children to read the word.
		  • Ask them to tell you which picture matches the word by holding up the appropriate number of fingers.
		
		Read the sentence
		• Ask the children to read aloud as you point to the words.
		• Read the sentence together.
		• Tell the children to read the sentence one more time.

A word about the schwa

The schwa is the name for the most common sound in English. It is the unstressed sound that we find in many words; it makes an 'uh' sound, which varies according to accent. For example, the 'o' in 'lesson' makes the schwa sound. The phonemic symbol for the schwa is ə. Schwa can be represented in writing by all five vowels, and by a number of digraphs and trigraphs such as 'er', 'ou', 'or' and 'our'.

Introducing the schwa in Phase 3
Children first meet the schwa in Phase 3 when they read words ending in 'er'. In many accents the 'er' makes an unstressed vowel sound at the end of words such as 'bigger' and 'better', but in other accents these words are pronounced with pure sounds.

The schwa in two-syllable words in Phases 3 and 4
Later in Phase 3 and in Phase 4, children will encounter some two-syllable words with the schwa sound that do not have the 'er' ending. Words such as 'dragon' and 'frighten' can be read using the GPCs the children know and with the chunking technique.

1) Say the word with pure sounds, a syllable at a time, for example: d-r-a-g/o-n.

2) Modify the pronunciation of the word. **Say:** *But we say dragən (with the schwa).*

3) Teach vocabulary. **Say:** *A dragon is a monster that breathes fire. It is not a real animal. It only appears in stories.*

The schwa in Phase 5
Many combinations of vowels can make the schwa sound, especially in longer words. In Phase 5, the 'er' in 'spider', the first 'o' in 'potato', the 'e' in 'oven' and the 'a' in 'giant' make the schwa! Once again, it all depends on accent. We teach children to read these words with the chunking method and pure sounds, and then how the word is said (in their accent) with the schwa. This is important as so many words have the schwa!

The table below gives example words containing the schwa sound from the Little Wandle SEND programme.

Phase 3	Phase 4	Phase 5
better bigger ever finger	printer swimmer trainers children dragon frighten monster	avenue human sofa spider potato giant oven potion magician

Precision teaching grids

Phase 2 grapheme chart

If the child cannot make accurate speech sounds, accept the sounds they make.

Grapheme card	Picture card	Objects for What's in the box?	Pronunciation phrase
		sock sun star snake	Show your teeth and let the **s** hiss out **ssssss ssssss**
		ant apple arrow astronaut	Open your mouth wide and make the **a** sound at the back of your mouth **a a a**
		teddy toast teeth tiger	Open your lips; put the tip of your tongue behind your teeth and press **t t t**
		pencil pizza peg penguin	Bring your lips together, push them open and say **p p p**
		insect invitation igloo iguana	Pull your lips back and make the **i** sound at the back of your mouth **i i i**
		nurse nose nest net	Open your lips a bit; put your tongue behind your teeth and make the **nnnnn** sound **nnnnn**
		moon marble monkey mouse	Put your lips together and make the **mmmmm** sound **mmmmm**
		dog door dinosaur duck	Put your tongue to the top and front of your mouth and make a quick **d** sound **d d d**
		grapes glue glasses goat	Give me a big smile that shows your teeth; press the middle of your tongue to the top and back of your mouth; push your tongue down and forward to make the **g** sound **g g g**
		orange otter ostrich octopus	Make your mouth into a round shape and say **o o o**

Grapheme card	Picture card	Objects for What's in the box?	Pronunciation phrase
c		car cup crown cat	Open your mouth into a little smile; make your tongue flat and move it up towards the top of your mouth to say **c c c**
k		kangaroo kettle ketchup kite	Open your mouth into a little smile; make your tongue flat and move it up towards the top of your mouth to say **k k k**
ck		neck lock tick sock	Open your mouth into a little smile; make your tongue flat and move it up towards the top of your mouth to say **c c c**
e		egg elbow envelope elephant	Open your mouth wide and say **e e e**
u		under (something under a table) upset umbrella	Open your mouth wide and say **u u u**
r		rocket rabbit rice rainbow	Show me your teeth to make a **rrrr** sound **rrrrr**
h		hat hammer house helicopter	Open your mouth and breathe out sharply **h h h**
b		ball bus bird bear	Put your lips together and say **b** as you open them **b b b**
f		fish frog flower flamingo	Open your lips a little; put your teeth on your bottom lip and push the air out to make the sound **fffff fffff**
l		leaf lips lemon lollipop	Open your mouth a little; put your tongue up to the top of your mouth, behind your teeth, and press **lllll lllll**
j		jam jug jellyfish	Pucker your lips and show your teeth; use your tongue as you say **j j j**

Grapheme card	Picture card	Objects for What's in the box?	Pronunciation phrase
v		volcano van vegetable	Put your teeth against your bottom lip and make a buzzing sound **vvvvv vvvvv**
w		wave wig web	Pucker your lips and keep them small as you say **w w w**
x		box fox wax (candle)	Mouth open, then push the **cs/x** sound through as you close your mouth **cs cs cs** (**x x x**)
y		yoyo yellow yap (dog)	Smile, tongue to the top of your mouth; say **y** without opening your mouth **y y y**
z		zebra zip zoo	Show me your teeth and buzz the **z** sound **zzzzz zzzzz**
qu		queen quack (duck) quick (action)	Pucker your mouth, then open it as you say **qu qu qu**
ch		No more objects for the games.	Pucker your lips and show your teeth; use your tongue as you say **ch ch ch**
sh			Show me your teeth and push the air out **shshshshshsh**
th			Voiced: Tongue on your teeth, teeth almost closed to make a 'buzzing' **th th th** Unvoiced: Tongue on your teeth, push the air out **th th th**
ng			Open your mouth a bit and then use your tongue at the back of your mouth to say **ng ng ng**
nk			Open your mouth a bit and then use your tongue at the back of your mouth to say **nk nk nk**

Phase 3 grapheme chart

If the child cannot make accurate speech sounds, accept the sounds they make.

Grapheme	Catchphrase	Pronunciation phrase
ai	tail in the rain	Open your mouth wide and say **ai ai ai**
ee	sheep in a jeep	Smile with your lips apart and say **ee ee ee**
igh	a light in the night	Open your mouth in a relaxed way and say **igh igh igh**
oa	soap that goat	Make an 'o' with your mouth and say **oa oa oa**

Grapheme	Catchphrase	Pronunciation phrase
oo	hook a book	Pucker your lips and keep them small as you say **oo oo oo**
oo	zoom to the moon	Open your mouth just a bit, put your hand on your tummy, pull your tummy in and say **oo oo oo**
ar	march in the dark	Open your mouth wide, push your tongue down and say **ar ar ar**
or	born with a horn	Make an 'o' with your mouth, push your tongue down and say **or or or**

Grapheme	Catchphrase	Pronunciation phrase
ur	curl the fur	Open your mouth in a relaxed way, push your tongue down and say **ur ur ur**
ow	wow owl	Open your mouth wide then move your lips together as you say **ow ow ow**
oi	boing boing	Make an 'o' with your mouth then move your lips out as you say **oi oi oi**

Grapheme	Catchphrase	Pronunciation phrase
ear	get near to hear	Smile with your lips apart, push your tongue to your teeth as you say **ear ear ear**
air	chair in the air	Open your mouth wide, push your tongue down as you say **air air air**
er	a bigger digger	Open your mouth in a relaxed way, push your tongue down and say **ur ur ur**

Phase 5 grapheme chart

If the child cannot make accurate speech sounds, accept the sounds they make.

Grapheme and phoneme	Picture	Pronunciation phrase	Grapheme and phoneme	Picture	Pronunciation phrase
ay /ai/	crayons	Open your mouth wide and say **ai ai ai**	ir /ur/	bird	Open your mouth in a relaxed way, push your tongue down and say **ur ur ur**
ou /ow/	cloud	Open your mouth wide then move your lips together as you say **ow ow ow**	ie /igh/	pie	Open your mouth in a relaxed way and say **igh igh igh**
oy /oi/	toy	Make an 'o' with your mouth, then move your lips out as you say **oi oi oi**	ue /oo/	blue	Pucker your lips and keep them small as you say oo oo oo
ea /ee/	beach	Smile with your lips apart and say **ee ee ee**	ue /yoo/	statue	Pucker your lips and keep them small as you say **yoo yoo yoo**

Grapheme and phoneme	Picture	Pronunciation phrase	Grapheme and phoneme	Picture	Pronunciation phrase
u /yoo/	unicorn	Pucker your lips and keep them small as you say **yoo yoo yoo**	e /ee/	lemur	Smile with your lips apart and say **ee ee ee**
o /oa/	robot	Make an 'o' with your mouth and say **oa oa oa**	ow /oa/	rainbow	Make an 'o' with your mouth and say **oa oa oa**
i /igh/	spider	Open your mouth in a relaxed way and say **igh igh igh**	a–e /ai/	cake	Open your mouth wide and say **ai ai ai**
a /ai/	apron	Open your mouth wide and say **ai ai ai**	i–e /igh/	bike	Open your mouth in a relaxed way and say **igh igh igh**

|

Grapheme and phoneme	Picture	Pronunciation phrase
o–e /oa/	fishbone	Make an 'o' with your mouth and say **oa oa oa**
u–e /yoo/	tubes	Pucker your lips and keep them small as you say **yoo yoo yoo**
e–e /ee/	athlete	Smile with your lips apart and say **ee ee ee**
ew /oo/	jewels	Pucker your lips and keep them small as you say oo oo oo

Grapheme and phoneme	Picture	Pronunciation phrase
ie /ee/	shield	Smile with your lips apart and say **ee ee ee**
aw /or/	paws	Make an 'o' with your mouth, push your tongue down and say **or or or**
ea /e/	bread	Open your mouth wide and say **e e e**
y /ee/	jelly	Smile with your lips apart and say **ee ee ee**

Grapheme and phoneme	Picture	Pronunciation phrase	Grapheme and phoneme	Picture	Pronunciation phrase
wh /w/ **wh**eel		Pucker your lips and keep them small as you say **w w w**	c /s/ mi**c**e		Show your teeth and let the **s** hiss out **sssssss**
y /igh/ butter**fl**y		Open your mouth in a relaxed way and say **igh igh igh**	ph /f/ ele**ph**ant		Open your lips a little; put your teeth on your bottom lip and push the air out to make the sound **fffff**
g /j/ **g**iant		Pucker your lips and show your teeth; use your tongue as you say **j j j**	are /air/ squ**are**		Open your mouth wide, push your tongue down and say **air air air**
dge /j/ bri**dge**		Pucker your lips and show your teeth; use your tongue as you say **j j j**	se /z/ chee**se**		Show me your teeth and buzz the **z** sound **zzzzz zzzzz**

Grapheme and phoneme	Picture	Pronunciation phrase
le /l/	apple	Open your mouth a little; put your tongue up to the top of your mouth, behind your teeth, and press lllll lllll
ve /v/	leaves	Put your teeth against your bottom lip and make a buzzing sound vvvvv vvvvv
o /u/	gloves	Open your mouth wide and say u u u
a /o/	watch	Make your mouth into a round shape and say o o o

Grapheme and phoneme	Picture	Pronunciation phrase
a /or/	ball	Make an 'o' with your mouth, push your tongue down and say or or or
ti /sh/	station	Show me your teeth and push the air out shshshshshsh
ci /sh/	magician	Show me your teeth and push the air out shshshshshsh
ore /or/	snore	Make an 'o' with your mouth, push your tongue down and say or or or

SEND core graphemes with more than one sound

a	**a**stronaut	**a**pron	ea	b**ea**ch	br**ea**d
e	**e**lephant	l**e**mur	ie	p**ie**	sh**ie**ld
i	**i**guana	sp**i**der	y	**y**oyo	jell**y**
o	**o**ctopus	r**o**bot	c	**c**at	mi**c**e
u	**u**mbrella	**u**nicorn	g	**g**oat	**g**iant
ow	**ow**l	rainb**ow**			